Showers of Grass-hoppers

AND OTHER MIRACLE STORIES FROM AFRICA

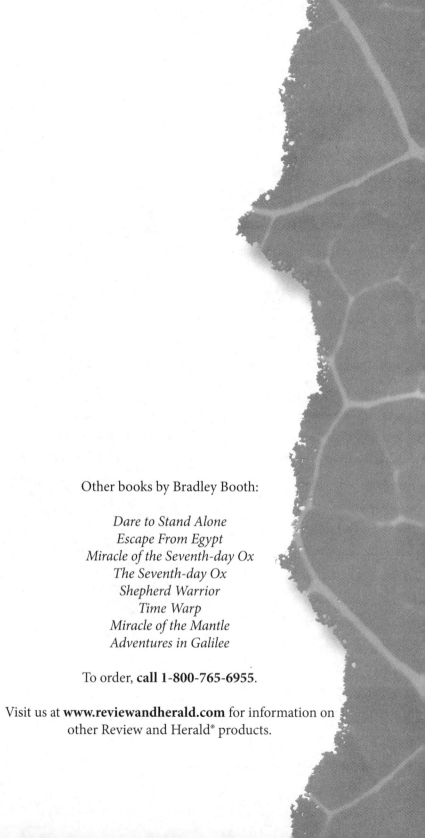

Other books by Bradley Booth:

Dare to Stand Alone
Escape From Egypt
Miracle of the Seventh-day Ox
The Seventh-day Ox
Shepherd Warrior
Time Warp
Miracle of the Mantle
Adventures in Galilee

To order, **call 1-800-765-6955**.

Visit us at **www.reviewandherald.com** for information on
other Review and Herald® products.

BRADLEY BOOTH

Showers of Grass-hoppers

AND OTHER MIRACLE STORIES FROM AFRICA

REVIEW AND HERALD® PUBLISHING ASSOCIATION
Since 1861 | www.reviewandherald.com

Published by Review and Herald® Publishing Association, Hagerstown, MD 21741-1119

Review and Herald® titles may be purchased in bulk for educational, business, fund-raising, or sales promotional use. For information, e-mail SpecialMarkets@reviewandherald.com.

The Review and Herald® Publishing Association publishes biblically based materials for spiritual, physical, and mental growth and Christian discipleship.

The author assumes full responsibility for the accuracy of all facts and quotations as cited in this book.

Unless otherwise noted, Bible texts in this book are from the New King James Version. Copyright © 1979, 1980, 1982 by Thomsas Nelson, Inc. Used by permission. All rights reserved.

Bible texts credited to TNIV are from the *Holy Bible, Today's New International Version.* Copyright 2001, 2005 by International Bible Society. Used by permission of International Bible Society. All rights reserved worldwide.

This book was
Edited by Kalie Kelch
Copyedited by Delma Miller
Designed by Emily Ford / Review and Herald® Design Center
Cover art by Emily Ford / © Thinkstock.com
Typeset: Minion Pro 11/13

PRINTED IN U.S.A.

17 16 15 14 13   5 4 3 2 1

Library of Congress Cataloging-in-Publication Data
Booth, Bradley, 1957- .
Showers of grasshoppers and other miracle stories from Africa / Bradley
Booth.
   p. cm.
1. Miracles—Africa. I. Title.
 BT97.3.B67 2013
 286.7'66—dc23
               2012032261

ISBN 978-0-8280-2653-6

Dedication

This book is dedicated to the faithful ones on the continent of Africa who have let their light shine for Jesus. Service in the small things of life prepared them for the big challenges of witnessing for God when times seemed the hardest. Of one thing they were sure: the Bible is the Word of God, and He is faithful and just to fulfill all the promises He has given His children.

SHOWERS
OF GRASSHOPPERS

Chapter 1

"The year was a dry one," Grandpa Manu muttered, scratching his scraggly gray beard as he told a story from years gone by. "It was a bad time for everyone, especially the farmers! The rains hadn't come for weeks, and my father was worried that we would lose the few crops we had managed to keep alive."

The old man straightened his back a moment to stare at the circle of faces sitting around the evening fire. "Of course, when the farmers suffer, so does everyone else in the village," he added. "Crops have always been the most important part of village life in Nigeria. No crops? No money for the basics in life. No maize to make sour kenkey. No beans or tomatoes to sell in the market so we can buy medicine or a colorful dress for Mama to wear at festivals.

"I was just a young man of 7, but even I knew trouble was coming. There would be little we could do that year to satisfy the gnawing hunger in the pit of our stomachs. There was only the hard, twisted roots of the shriveled cassava plants, and cassava can get pretty boring when that's all there is for a boy to eat.

"And that was it. Without rain no one could hold out any hope for the farmers, not even the village chieftain, or babalawo, as we called him." Grandpa Manu had a faraway look in his eyes as he stared into the evening fire. "'The spirits are angry!' we were told at a village meeting, and who could argue with the babalawo and his shaman? That's what we had always believed. There were more than 400 Yoruban spirits in our religion, and we were sure one of them must be angry enough to bring us the drought!" Grandpa frowned at the weird shadows cast by the flickering firelight. "Our fears took over, and the shaman made sure of it!"

A cascade of sparks jumped into the air as Manu's son, Danso, threw some branches from the jaree hiji tree on the evening fire. Flames of yellow, orange, and red jumped to life, giving the fire added brightness. Moths and flying beetles emerged from the overgrowth of vegetation near the campfire, drawn irresistibly to the dancing firelight. The curious little insects fluttered as near the light of the flames as they could, as near as they dared without being scorched by the radiating heat. Now and then one would fly too close, singe its fragile wings, and be caught in the updraft rising from the crackling fire.

Danso stared at his father over the firelight as the story continued. He didn't feel at ease listening to his father speak of evil omens, but when Manu got past the frightening parts, the stories were quite entertaining. Storytelling was part of their family traditions, something that was culturally passed from father to son. It was an art, and Danso knew sooner or later he would be called to carry on the tradition, since he was the oldest of Manu's sons.

"We thought the drought was bad," Grandpa Manu said, "and then more disaster struck!" His eyes grew big and his hands moved in animated gestures. "A plague of grasshoppers descended on our village like no one had ever seen! It was a sight to behold and quite scary for me! I was just a small boy and had never seen such a thing! There were scads of 'em everywhere, like the sands of the sea! So many you couldn't count 'em! They swarmed in and covered the countryside like a blanket! They crawled over the roads and pathways by the millions. We couldn't walk anywhere without stepping on 'em! They landed on the fields and weighed the branches of the trees down so heavy the limbs started breaking off! It was awful!" Grandpa said, his voice getting squeaky. "They were like machines. They ate every green leaf and stalk and plant in sight, until they left the countryside desolate!

"No one knew what to do!" Grandpa paused for a moment. "All we knew was what the local babalawo had told us. 'You need to give offerings to the shaman!' he said again and again. 'Otherwise the grasshoppers will eat everything, and then times will be hard for a long, long time.'"

Danso tried to imagine such a scourge, but it was difficult. At 35 he knew only the stories his father and the other old men of the village told around the evening campfires. This particular story was a familiar one, and he had heard it scores of times. But each time he heard the frightening tale, he felt as if he were hearing it for the first time. In his mind's eye he could see the grasshoppers crawling everywhere like a squirming, creeping carpet! He could almost feel the crunching, moving bodies of the insects under his feet!

The children around the fire relived those moments too. Their eyes widened with wonder and fear at the thought of a grasshopper plague. The story Grandpa Manu told was no more real to them right now than a sea monster, but you wouldn't have known it by the looks on their faces. Luami and little Abu, Danso's smallest children, couldn't take their eyes off Grandpa as he added detail after detail to the horrific story. Even 15-year-old Motumba seemed mesmerized as he listened to the frightening tale from long ago.

Danso was proud of his family. Abena was a good wife who had given him three healthy children. He had a small farm, which provided for his family's needs. Their one-room house was small, but it was adequate. Actually, it was more like a hut, but they owned it and the land on which it stood in the savanna of the semi-arid lands of West Africa. The hut was made of mud brick walls with one window that opened to the morning sun. Best of all, Danso had his health. He was strong and had never been sick a day in his life, something he had inherited no doubt from his father, Grandpa Manu.

Grandpa lived in a little hut out behind Danso's house in a grove of coconut palms. He was getting on in years, but he liked his independence and insisted on keeping his own house. And Abena understood that, though she did send Luami over to his house nearly every day now with a pot of cornmeal kenkey or beans or cassava.

As Danso listened to Grandpa's story, he knew he was blessed. Times had been good. He knew nothing of grasshopper plagues or drought. His crops were usually very good! Danso was sure the good spirits were part of the reason, but he had to admit there were fears in his heart too. Fear of evil spirits ruled the village like an iron fist, and Danso was never sure when his streak of good luck would end. Without doubt the babalawo and his village shaman were the religious gurus in the Nigerian town of Babban Zugu. Everyone called the shaman "Father of the Mysteries" and "Father of the Spirits." Danso didn't want to admit it, but he was as much afraid of the shaman as anyone in town.

The flames were burning low once again for lack of fuel, and Grandpa Manu stared into the fire as if that might keep it burning a little bit longer. "We were all scared of the Babalawo's prophecy about the grasshoppers, and with good reason!" Grandpa's eyes grew wide again. "He was right in his prediction! The devastation from the grasshopper hordes was terrible! We just stood there watching the little monsters gobble up every growing thing in sight! When they had finished, not a speck of green could be seen anywhere! Nothing! It was all gone, and then they rose in gigantic swarms and flew away on the eastern wind!"

No one said anything more for the longest time after Grandpa ended his story. Luami was nodding off, and little Abu was already sleeping in his mother's arms.

"Do you think it's possible we could see such a plague this year?" Danso finally asked.

Grandpa Manu shrugged. "Who can say? It's dry this year, and we've seen plenty of grasshoppers around, but it usually takes at least two seasons of drought to bring the worst of the little pests. Of course, the weather we're having here in Nigeria may be different from what they're having in regions north and east of here toward the desert. That would definitely make a difference."

The old man stood to his feet and rubbed the back of his neck. "Well, tomorrow is another day. We'd better get some sleep. Our bean field won't plant itself. When we're finished we should probably carry water from the well to water the plants. It'll take time, but with the weather turning drier, it's the only way to be sure the beans will ripen in time." He stared up at the night sky. "I wish we had a way to irrigate our fields. There's got to be a way to get water to our fields more easily."

"There probably is," Danso replied sleepily as he picked up Luami and headed for the house with Abena. "We'll figure it out next year."

Chapter 2

Danso woke the next morning to the cooing of doves in the coconut palms along the river bottom. Before the coppery sun had emerged from its bed below the milky horizon, the young farmer was hitching his plow to the old ox. Breakfast had not even been served, but he hoped to get a bit of ground turned before the sun got too hot. He would come in later to get a bite to eat. These cool morning temperatures seemed too good to just sit around like a lazy man in his house.

A pair of lizards raced along ahead of Danso as he slapped the reins on the broad back of the ox. "Get up, there, Suki!" he called as Suki dragged the plow out to the patch of ground they were preparing for seed. The field was already partially turned from his work the day before. With some luck he'd be able to turn the rest of the soil by noon. It wasn't a large tract. Just two hectares (five acres) in size, but the beans he planted there, if the spirits wished it, would be enough to give him the money he needed to support his family. He didn't need much. It was his children he was most concerned about. School fees for the two older children were a must, and uniforms, and maybe even shoes, if things went especially well. Beans were usually a good cash crop, and this patch of yellow clay soil had grown good beans before.

After an hour or so, Motumba, his oldest son, and Grandpa Manu came out and cleared the weeds and brambles that had gotten a foothold in the soil since the last planting. They all worked quickly, taking time only for a short meal of rice and cassava partway through the morning.

The soil wasn't too hard, and by noon Danso had accomplished his goal—the ground was ready for planting. Biting flies buzzed everywhere, and only Suki's swishing tail and Danso's willow switch kept them from biting Suki mercilessly. Scores of grasshoppers jumped across their pathway as they headed for the house to unhitch the wooden plow. The sun was straight overhead, but Danso and Suki had already put in a day's work.

While Motumba took old Suki to the river for a well-deserved drink, Danso checked the bean seed he had been preparing for the next planting. The previous night he had put the seed into a large calabash gourd full of water to let them soak. Soaking the seed was an old trick he used to get the seeds ready for planting. "Keeps them moist for days so they have a chance of sprouting faster," he told Motumba when the boy came back from the river with Suki.

Then they all went inside to escape the torturing African sun. It was too hot to work and too hot to eat. It was even too hot to sleep. The air inside the house was stifling, and everyone finally had to carry their mats outside to take a nap in the shade of the trees.

By 3:00 p.m. the temperatures were bearable again, and the men went back outside to work.

"I say there, brother, could I trouble you for a cup of cool water?" a tall handsome stranger called from the road. "I've walked quite a distance today, and a little shade would feel nice about now."

"Absolutely," Danso smiled in greeting. "Bring the man some water," he called to Motumba, and then he invited the stranger to sit in the shade of a mango tree. "What brings you our way?" Danso asked, more for the sake of conversation than anything.

"My name is Kossi. I'm bringing good news to all the farmers in this area," the stranger said cheerfully.

"Good news? I could do with some of that right now," Danso half smiled while running his hand through the gourdful of seeds waiting to be planted. "The soil is right for planting, but we can only guess what the weather will do. Last year was a wet one, and the corn I planted sat in pools of water for weeks. It was a poor harvest, and I didn't have money for school fees, so my daughter had to miss school until the next crop came in. And of course there was no money for extras. Anybody getting sick with malaria had to do without the government chloroquine."

The stranger frowned. "I'm sorry to hear of your misfortune. Farming is hard enough without things going wrong to threaten your crops." He smiled at Motumba when the boy arrived with a large cup of cool water.

"Yes, well, that is the luck of things with farmers. The only thing we can count on is that there is always some risk." Danso watched the stranger finish his water. "And now you must excuse me, friend," he added, as Grandpa Manu came out of the house. "We have much to do before the sun sets today."

"Need any help?" The handsome young man set down his traveling book bag.

Danso stopped in surprise. "You want to work in the fields?"

"Why not? I've done my share of planting while growing up. You need the help, and the day waits for no one."

"Well now, you speak the truth," Danso laughed, "and you have a sense of humor."

And so the four of them went to work in the fields, the afternoon rays of the sun turning their sweaty bodies into shimmering shadows of heat. The work went fast with the four of them working. They talked of crops and weather and government news. In no time at all they had finished planting four long rows of beans and reached the shade at the edge of the field.

"The bean crops in this field have always been good," Danso straightened up and leaned on his planting stick. "It was a bean crop from this field that gave me the money I needed to finally choose a wife. How about you? Have you any plans to marry?" Danso grinned at Kossi with a twinkle in his eye.

"No, I guess I'm too busy doing the Lord's work," Kossi smiled shyly as he stopped to rest too. "I have no time for a wife right now." Danso guessed there was probably more to this story than a busy schedule. Starting a family was expensive. If a young man wanted to get married, he had to first prove that he could support a wife. That meant he had to be able to earn enough money to pay a bride-price for a woman he considered ideal for marriage. That in turn meant he had to impress the young woman's parents. But a bride-price was only the beginning.

Several types of ceremonies were necessary to get married, which got expensive. Government ceremonies were a matter of formality with the couple paying a fee before registering their names at the regional office. Christian or Muslim marriages took on a deeper significance because the couple was asking for God's blessing on their marriage, and that usually required a feast of celebration. But it was the elaborate traditional village wedding in Nigeria that cost the most, and a young man without money or means couldn't afford this ceremony.

"Where are you from?" Grandpa Manu asked, wiping the sweat from his brow.

"I'm a student at the Seventh-day Adventist Seminary in Lagos," Kossi replied. "Our instructors teach us how to sell books and give Bible studies. I'm on the road all the time now selling books so I can earn a scholarship to go to school and become a minister."

"Tell me about your books." Danso marked off the next four rows and then started planting seeds again. "These books must be good indeed for you to give up plans for a family right away."

"It's true; the books are the best! They have the words of life in them, and I get so excited when I show them to people!" Kossi had to hurry to keep up with Danso and Manu's pace. "I have books about how to be happy and stay healthy, and books about how to find the treasures of eternal life."

"Happy is good," Danso chuckled to himself, "but that part about treasure I could use." He stopped to stare at Kossi. "What kind of treasure are you talking about?"

Kossi stopped to wipe the sweat from his brow once again. "I'm talking about heavenly treasure. This earth is not much of a home, with all the troubles we have in it. We weren't made to live in a world like this, and someday soon God will come and take us to our home in heaven where all our troubles will end. No more hard times. No more droughts. No more weevils or grasshopper plagues."

"I'd like to hear more about that," Danso's voice grew serious. "I tend to look on the bright side of things, but I've had my fair share of sadness too. My wife and I lost our first child."

"These books can help with that too," Kossi smiled. "When you feel that there's no one to turn to, the books I have will remind you about a God who loves you. He will never leave you, never forsake you, never fail you in times of need. He's the same yesterday, today, and forever. Eternally kind, and merciful, and compassionate. He sent His Son, Jesus, to die for you, Danso, and He wants to help you live a full life here too."

Danso could tell by the look on Kossi's face that he really believed what he was saying, and that was a powerful testimony for a man like Danso, who had never believed in anything but the power of the spirits.

Chapter 3

The sun was getting low in the sky. Danso shaded his eyes as he looked to the west. "Well, I think we've done enough for today. I want to thank you for helping us with the work this afternoon. You are an unusual man." Danso reached out his dusty hand to take Kossi's. "Won't you stay for the evening meal? We haven't much, but what we have, we'll gladly share. You deserve that much."

"Thank you," Kossi grinned. "That's a fine offer."

"You must be a real man of faith," Danso said later as the men sat eating the rice and peanut sauce Abena had prepared for them. "Where did you get such spiritual strength?"

"I haven't always been like this," Kossi said humbly. "When I first arrived at the seminary, I didn't have any money, and I worried about whether God would care for me as He promised. I hadn't yet learned to trust the words of Jesus when He said, 'Look at the birds of the air, for they neither sow nor reap nor gather into barns; yet your heavenly Father feeds them. Are you not of more value than they?'" (Matt. 6:26).

Danso didn't think he had ever met a man quite like Kossi. He had an unusual look of peace and confidence in his eyes.

"And then one day my world came crashing down around me," Kossi continued. "I received a letter from home telling me my mother was very ill, and the chances of her recovering were getting slimmer every day. If she died and I didn't get to see her one last time, that would be unforgivable. My tribal culture requires that I go home to my village to pay the proper respects to my mother. But how was I to do that?" Kossi asked earnestly. "You see, I had no money and no hope of getting any soon.

"So I just sat there on my bed in the dormitory with my head in my hands. What was I to do? My job selling religious books didn't pay much. In fact, sometimes I had to go weeks without pay of any kind because the money I got for selling books was not regular. Each morning the other young men and I listened to lectures from our instructors at the seminary on how to give Bible studies and how to preach sermons. Then in the afternoon we usually went out to sell books and Bibles to the common folks on the street.

"And that was my big problem! I hadn't had much financial success lately. People were interested in the books, and sometimes they even purchased one or two, but no one had paid me for the sales I had made during the last week. I needed to revisit these homes, deliver the books, and try to collect the money.

"But now with no money I was in desperate straits. I needed about 1,500 naira [approximately 10 American dollars] to pay for the bus ride home to see my mother. But it might as well have been 150,000 naira for all the chance there was that I was going to be able to raise that kind of money. I'm a poor boy, and I had nothing!"

Kossi grinned at Danso in his boyish way. "And then I realized my mistake. I hadn't yet prayed about my problem. God could help me. I had just read about this very kind of problem in my Bible that morning. 'With God all things are possible,' the passage said [Matt. 19:26]. It's one of my favorite verses of Scripture now.

"And you know, I found myself believing it at that moment. All things are possible with God. My mind began turning, and I thought, *He's got many ways He can work this thing out for me. He can give me the money so I can go home, or He can help me sell books so I will have enough money to travel, or He can help my mother get well so I won't have to go home at all.*

"Dropping to my knees by my bed, I poured out my heart to God in simple faith. 'I'm sorry I didn't bring this to You in prayer earlier,' I told God. 'You own the cattle on a thousand hills, Lord, and this problem is just a tiny one for You. I know that prayer is the key to unlock heaven's storehouse. Please forgive me for my lack of faith. Help me to find the answer for this problem. Whatever way You choose to answer this prayer is OK with me.' And then I snatched up my satchel and left my room for an afternoon selling my books. I was doing my part, and now God could do His.

"All that afternoon I visited with interested folks who loved the books I was selling. Unfortunately, no one had money for my books. Then one family I visited asked me to explain from the Bible what happens to people after they die. My session with the family ran long, and before I realized it the sun was going down, and it was time to go home.

" 'Thank You, Lord, for helping me to find a family that is wanting to learn Your ways!' I prayed excitedly as I walked back to the seminary. And then suddenly I remembered that I still had no money for the bus fare back to my village. 'God will provide,' I told myself. 'He always has, and He won't fail me now.'

"When I arrived back at the seminary, I found the small kitchen empty. The evening meal was over, and there was only a little rice left in one pot. I sat down to eat it, but I began feeling a little bit sorry for myself. I hadn't made any sales that day; I hadn't collected any money from the delivery of the books; I had no money to travel back to see my mother; and now I had missed out on the main meal of the day, too."

Kossi paused in his story. By now Abena and Luami had come to stand in the doorway. They had eaten in the lean-to off the back of the house, but found Kossi's story too good to resist any longer.

"And then Mrs. Alima, the seminary director's wife, came in," Kossi continued. "I don't think she heard me arrive, because she looked startled. She laughed and gave me a motherly pat on the head. 'It's good to see you home safely, young man,' and then she handed me a letter that had just arrived that afternoon. When I opened the envelope, I was shocked, because 1,500 naira fell out, the exact amount I needed to travel home! I stared at the money in surprise. 'Thank You, Lord' was all I could whisper as I bowed my head reverently. 'Who brought the money?' " I asked.

"Mrs. Alima smiled. 'It was Neka Adeogun, a missionary woman from the church in Lagos. She said she felt impressed that you needed some money, so she brought it by.'

"My mouth dropped open in surprise. 'Praise God!' was all I could say. How could the missionary have known I needed exactly 1,500 naira? My mind was in a whirl, but Mrs. Alima had no answers, so I made preparations to go home immediately."

Danso could see the light in Kossi's shining eyes as he shared the miracle story. "Where did you get such faith?" he asked Kossi. "Such faith must be rare."

"Maybe," Kossi nodded. "But I think God gives each of us our own portion of faith. It's true I can't deny that getting the money was anything short of a miracle. But there is more to the story."

"The story's not finished?"

"It is not," Kossi smiled mysteriously. "The next morning I left on the bus and arrived in my village by late afternoon. I spent a wonderful week with my mother, and she recovered nicely, thanks be to God. At the end of the week I returned to Lagos in time to attend church the following Sabbath.

"During the service that day I stood to give my testimony about how God had answered my prayer, and the church gave me some hearty amens.

And then I heard the rest of the story from Mrs. Adeogun, the missionary woman who gave me the money. She had had a dream in which she saw I needed money for some problem. She didn't know exactly why I needed the money, but she decided to help me anyway. She ended up bringing me 1,500 naira, quite unaware that this was the exact amount of money I needed to go home to see my mother."

Kossi's eyes misted over as he told this part. "And so you see, Danso, God has been very good to me. He has taken care of my every need, and often in quite remarkable ways! I'll never doubt Him again."

The hour was late now. Nobody could keep their eyes open any longer, so they all stretched out on their sleeping mats on the floor. Kossi was now welcome among them because he had worked with them in their field and eaten a meal with them and shared his personal testimony.

At breakfast the next morning Kossi showed them his books, and Danso bought a big one called *Bible Readings for the Home*.

"I just happen to have an extra copy with me, so I can give you one right now," Kossi said with his usual grin. "That's a blessing! Now you won't have to wait several weeks for me to return with another copy."

Danso and Abena were impressed with Kossi and his life of self-sacrifice at the seminary. "Can you come again?" they asked. "We'd like to know more about a God who can do miracles like the ones He's done for you."

This was the beginning of a real friendship, one that would change Danso and Abena's life in the days to come. As the days stretched into weeks, the long rows of beans sprouted and grew, and Danso's family was kept busy watering and hoeing the young crop. But every morning and noon and night they found it convenient to stop their work and read from the book Kossi had sold them. Not surprisingly, the things they found in its pages were truly remarkable!

Chapter 4

Abena hummed a lively tune as she clipped weeds with her sharp hoe in the small patch that featured cassava, tomatoes, and cabbage plants. The late afternoon sun played tag with dappling shadows along the edge of the family vegetable garden as Abena worked, stopping from time to time to wipe the sweat from her face. Iridescent dragonflies darted here and there among the plants, and lazy clouds drifted overhead in a sky of blue.

"Look, Mama," Luami exclaimed excitedly. "See my little pet grasshopper? Isn't he sweet?" She held the green-legged insect up, and its long, narrow body seemed gigantic in Luami's two little hands.

"Yes, I'm sure he is." Abena continued hoeing.

"Can I name him, Mama?"

"That would be nice," Abena said matter-of-factly as she listened to her daughter's aimless chatter, but her mind was far away.

"I think I'll call him Goliath, since he's so large. He is big, isn't he, Mama?"

"Yes, dear."

"Mama, you haven't even looked at him yet." Luami was persistent.

Abena stopped hoeing and glanced at Luami. "Oh!" she caught her breath in surprise. "He is big, isn't he? I haven't seen one that large in a long while."

"Oh, there's lots of big ones, Mama," Luami prattled on. "Some are even bigger. They live by the house and over by the jungle. I even saw three big ones by baby Abu's sleeping mat. Those ones were *really* big!"

"Is that so? By Abu's mat, were they?" Abena tried to go back to her work, but she found herself glancing at Luami's grasshopper again and again. The size of the grasshopper worried her. And Luami had said there were lots more. Abena didn't recall grasshoppers of this size living in the area, and that might mean it had migrated from somewhere else.

She stopped hoeing and glanced at the brassy sky overhead. The weather was unusually hot, and she wiped her brow with the back of her hand again. If Luami's grasshopper was this big, it had matured early in the season and was sure to be a hefty eater. She glanced down at the cassava

21

plants she was hoeing, and flicked two grasshoppers off one of the plants. The family garden was fair game for grasshoppers of this size, and they were already eating the precious plants. There weren't a lot of the hoppers or locusts as they were often called, but they were here just the same. Today there was a hundred, but maybe tomorrow there would be a thousand.

"Can I bring Goliath inside the house, Mama?" Luami jarred Abena from her worried thoughts.

"No, let's leave him outside, Luami. You can put him in a clay pot by the front door if you want to keep him. Just turn it upside down so he can't get out."

Abena came to the end of her row of cassava plants. "We've done enough work for now, Luami. It's time for us to go to the house and start preparing the evening meal."

"Oh, Mama!"

"No fussing, Luami. You can come out and play with the grasshopper later."

"Oh, all right," Luami mumbled. "Come on, Abu," she called to her baby brother. "Let's get some grass for Goliath. He'll be safe here until we get back. Now you be good, Goliath," she said as she turned the pot upside down and poked some grass through a small hole for the grasshopper to munch on. "I've got to go get supper ready right now, but I'll come back just as soon as I finish. You won't be lonely, will you?"

"Luami, come!" Abena called again from the doorway to the house. "Leave the grasshopper, and bring baby Abu." She sighed as she stood for a moment watching her daughter toying with the huge grasshopper.

She was worried about Luami. The girl was already 12 years old, but she was small for her age, and she was more interested in grasshoppers and frogs and things boys loved doing than what was expected of girls. Most girls her age were already cooking the rice and kokonte, a kind of paté made from cassava. Most were looking at boys and thinking about what it would be like to start a dowry and get married. Luami helped take care of 3-year-old Abu every day, but it was just a chore. Her heart was not really in it. Would she never be interested in such things?

Housework and having a family could be drudgery for any girl, but it was the life of every woman. However, Abena was certain marriage would not be a good fit for Luami so early in life. She was different. Abena didn't see the natural motherly instincts that should be growing in Luami's little heart if she was ever to be a mother. Other girls were often married by 14 or 15 years of age, but maybe God had something else in store for Luami. Could it be He didn't want her shouldering the responsibilities of a family this early in life like other girls?

Abena realized that God was creeping into her thoughts more and more since the family had been reading from the book Kossi had sold them. She felt that her faith was the size of a mustard seed, but it was growing. She just hoped that she could fully trust God with her daughter's future.

But Abena knew her husband was a traditional man when it came to women. Most men in the town of Babban Zugu were like that. "Girls belong in the home, and Luami is no different," Danso had said many, many times. "That is a woman's place. Luami should be helping you tend the house. What young man will want to marry Luami if she can't cook or take care of babies?"

Abena felt troubled every time she heard her husband talk like that. But even in the midst of her troubles, new thoughts kept stirring in her. Now that she and her family knew what it meant to be a Christian, things could never be the same for them. A new view on life had emerged for them, and the days ahead for their children seemed to be part of it. She didn't know exactly what all that might mean, but Luami's future was on her mind right now.

Abena had heard that in other parts of the world young girls were not expected to do so much while still so young. Places such as Europe and the United States allowed a girl to go to school and get an education before they had to start a home and become a mother. *Why can't Nigeria be more like that?* she thought as she remembered her own upbringing. She had accepted her life as a young teen bride because that's what young girls were taught to do. That's the way it was in rural West Africa, but at the start she had resented it just the same.

Now she was happy to have a family and keep house for her husband and children. And she loved their little farm, even with the many tasks that farming required. But Luami? Abena lay awake many nights worrying about Luami.

Abena snapped back to reality and stirred the coals of the fire in the little clay oven. "Can you pound the rest of the cassava and set it to boil, Luami? I'll make some more peanut sauce, and we can heat the rest of the rice we had last night. Hurry now, the sun is getting low in the sky. We don't want to keep the men waiting. They'll be hungry when they come in from the field."

Luami cheerfully put her hand to the task. She took the basket of cassava out back of the house where the tall wooden pestle sat upright in the mortar made from a hollowed-out chunk of wood. Pestles and mortars were used to pound many food stuffs in West Africa such as maize, millet, and root vegetables such as yams and manioc. Today she would pound the large tubers of manioc, or cassava, as some liked to call it.

Cutting up the first of the cassava, Luami threw it into the mortar and then grabbed the long wooden pestle in her little hands. Lifting the stout pole high over her head, she jumped into the air and brought the pestle down inside the mortar with all the force her little body could muster. She wasn't a big girl, but she had done this sort of work all her life, and she knew how to get the most out of her little arms and legs. "Use the weight of your body to help you, and you'll have to do less work," Abena always told her.

That was the way of life for village women in Nigeria. Besides the washing of clothes, food preparation took the most work. Growing the food was hard enough with its backbreaking hoeing and harvesting, not to mention the sweating, dirt under the fingernails, and calluses on the hands. And of course the food had to be prepared for cooking, which is where the pestle and mortar came in. Last of all it had to be cooked over an open fire, and that was a really sweaty job.

It was all hard work, but families had to eat. Poor families could not afford to eat much, but Abena's family grew most of their own food, so they usually ate pretty well. For breakfast they usually ate a little rice and maybe some beans or maize kenkey. They ate little or nothing during the hottest part of the day, but supper was their biggest meal. That was when a family could eat a whole pot of rice and peanut sauce made with spices, and maybe even some chicken or fish for special occasions, if they could get any. Motumba, their oldest son, sometimes brought fish home from the river, which was always a treat.

The climate of Nigeria was quite hot year-round. Certain times of the year it rained every day, and other times it would get very dry. Some years the crops grew well in the fields and gardens, but some years there was less rain, and then there wasn't much to eat.

Twice a year Abena and Danso would plant and harvest a crop and sell it in the village markets nearby. Vegetables were common crops, and this year's field of green beans were doing quite well. The beans were sure to be a bumper crop if the weather held up and didn't turn too dry. Already some of the bean plants had little blossoms on them, which meant the beans would be coming on shortly.

At the moment, Danso and Motumba were in an adjoining field hoeing the beans the family had planted five weeks earlier. Grandpa Manu was with them too, doing his part to support the family. He was more than 70 now, but he was still quite strong and wanted to carry his fair share of the workload.

The farm was a family enterprise. Everyone had a hand in its success, and everyone shared in the work of planting, hoeing, weeding, and harvesting the crop. The men did the regular work in the fields, but Abena did her part too when there was much to be done. Even Luami helped out, though she usually had to stay near the house to care for little Abu.

Besides caring for her brother and pounding the manioc, Luami's jobs around the house included fanning the cooking fire, cooking the meals, doing the laundry, and sweeping the front step and walkway to their house. There was always work to be done, but mostly Luami liked to play, and Abena saw to it that she got some time to do just that. She didn't have store-bought toys, but sometimes Grandpa Manu or Motumba would make her little dolls out of corn husks or mango leaves. Instead, her usual toys were just sticks and rocks and frogs, and of course, her pet grasshopper.

Chapter 5

The cool of day had come once again and with it the cry of loons down by the river. Colorful butterflies flitted along the slanting shafts of light as the afternoon sun dipped behind the row of trees bordering the family gardens.

"The men are coming in from the field!" Luami shouted as she danced through the open doorway.

"Good," Abena smiled tiredly. "The meal is ready."

All day the men had worked hoeing the long rows of beans. The beans were coming along nicely now, thanks to everyone's help in clearing out the weeds and making sure the plants got enough water. They also had to watch for bugs, snails, and other creatures that would eat up the crop before it had a chance to be harvested.

In West Africa plagues of caterpillars and bugs could multiply quickly and invade the fields of crops if untended, and that meant Danso and his family had to work all the harder. Keeping the pesky insects under control was a tough job. Danso couldn't afford the sprays or powdered chemicals big farmers used to keep the insects away, so he and the others usually walked the rows of beans and picked the bugs off the plants by hand. If the bugs became too bad, even Abena and Luami helped.

Motumba and the two men arrived at the house, washed up, and then seated themselves on the floor. The men usually ate their meal first. Abena and Luami would eat their meal later in the lean-to kitchen as was the custom for West African women.

"The food smells great!" Danso crowed as Luami dished up some rice and peanut sauce. "You women did yourself proud," he bragged, rubbing his tired eyes. "What do you think, Abu?" Danso pulled little Abu onto his lap. "Did they do a good job on the rice?" Little Abu only grinned as he began pushing rice into his mouth, but it was plain to see he loved being with his papa.

"That's the last of the cassava," Abena announced with a tired smile. "The cassava in the garden isn't ready to harvest yet, but I guess we can make maize kenkey to go with our rice for some of our meals. Until the beans are ready to pick, we won't have money to buy any extra things to cook with."

"That's fine by me," Danso said, smiling. "I like maize kenkey. I've been eating it all my life, and I'm not tired of it yet. It'll be nice to have some beans to eat and to sell, but for now you're still the best cook in Nigeria, no matter what's on the table."

"Thank you, Papa," Abena nodded and smiled in appreciation. Danso was a good husband who complimented her from time to time. Such a thing was uncommon in Africa, and Abena knew it.

"Can we read some more from the book Kossi brought us?" Luami asked, her eyes bright in anticipation. "I like the stories and all the questions in the book."

"That sounds like a good idea." Danso gave Luami a wink. "But first, why don't we pray and ask a blessing on the food before Motumba and Grandpa starve to death." Everybody laughed, and then they all bowed their heads.

"Thank You, Lord, for every good thing from above," Danso prayed. "We humbly ask that You bless this food. Thank You for the book Kossi brought us that has opened our eyes to You. Everything is so different now that we know about You. Bless our home, Lord, bless our bean crop. You know we need those beans so that we can send the children to school. And it would be nice for them to have shoes this year, too, Lord. God, hear our prayer. Amen."

No one said much during the meal, mostly because they were hungry, but also because that is the custom in sub-Saharan Africa. Eating is not considered a time for talking and socialization. At least not at the start of the meal. But later as their bellies filled and they began to relax, the conversation turned to events of the day.

"There sure are a lot of grasshoppers around this year," Motumba said as he ate the last of his rice.

"I've seen lots of them!" Luami added excitedly from the doorway of the lean-to kitchen. "There's green ones, and fat yellow ones, and big brown ones, but I think Goliath is the biggest one I've found yet."

"Luami, come here," Abena called from the kitchen. "Don't bother the men while they're eating."

"She's all right." Danso smiled at Luami. "And who is Goliath?"

Luami stepped out farther into the main room where the men were eating. "He's my pet grasshopper," she said proudly.

"A grasshopper!" Danso rolled his eyes in mock horror. "Honestly, child, why must you have a grasshopper for a pet? They're nothing but pests! They eat up our gardens and get into the well! They're nothing but a nuisance." But there was a twinkle in his eye as he stared lovingly at his daughter.

"I heard at the market that more and more grasshoppers are coming into the drier regions north of here," Grandpa Manu said. "I hope that's not a sign of bad things to come."

"Do you think they'll come this far south?" Motumba leaned back against the wall.

Danso frowned. "I hope not. Remember Grandpa's story, how the grasshoppers swarmed into the territory and ate every green thing in sight?" He shuddered. "I'd hate to think what would happen if the grasshoppers should come. Our bean crop is doing so well, and it will soon be ready to harvest, but just one day with a swarm of monsters like that and we'd be finished! They'd eat every bean in our field and leave nothing for us to live on till the next harvest!"

There was a long pause, and no one said anything as they thought about what Danso had said. Outside, the crickets had come to life, and little screech owls called to each other down by the river. Darkness had settled in for the night, and Abena lit a kerosene lamp to chase away the shadows.

"We must trust God," Abena said confidently. "He can protect our bean crop until it has been harvested. Nothing is too hard for God." She turned to Danso. "How much longer before we pick the beans to take them to the market?"

"Oh, 10 days until the first picking and then another week before the final picking. What do you think, Motumba?"

"That sounds about right," Motumba said, scratching his head. "Every part of the field has done well this year, so the harvest should be pretty even. Except, of course, that part over on the slope by the jungle. The ground is poor there."

"Do you think we can finish the hoeing tomorrow?"

Motumba thought for a moment. "If we hurry, maybe. For sure we can't afford to go back into the patch on Sunday because the blossoms are coming on. If we bump the plants, the blossoms might fall off, and then there will be no beans." It felt good having his father consult him about the crops as if he were one of the grown-ups.

"Good, then," Danso said, saluting Motumba. "We've got our work cut out for us."

After the meal Danso got out the book *Bible Readings for the Home,* and pulled the kerosene lamp closer so he could see. Grandpa Manu leaned against the wall to listen, and Motumba and Luami drew closer. Little Abu snuggled down into Abena's lap, content to spend the closing hours of the day safely tucked in his mother's arms with his family surrounding him.

Danso read to his family about the Bible being God's sure word of prophecy, about the signs of the times, and the three angels' messages of Revelation. He read about Creation and God's holy Sabbath, which was given as a memorial of that special week in earth's history. When he got to this part, Danso stopped and looked at Abena. "Listen to this," he said with a serious tone she had seldom heard before. "'Hallow My Sabbaths,'" he read, "'and they will be a sign between Me and you, that you may know that I am the Lord your God.' Ezekiel 20:20."

Danso read all there was in the chapter about the Sabbath. He was hungry for these gems of truth. He was thirsty for the words of life in this book. Finally he glanced at Abena and Grandpa Manu. "Tomorrow night the Sabbath begins," he said slowly, "and I aim to keep it. If God expects us to keep His Sabbath holy, then we need to do it. There'll be no more working here on the farm during God's Sabbath." He bowed his head. "It's the least we can do to obey God. We may not know everything in the Bible, but we know about the Sabbath now, and if we want God to bless us, we've got to begin keeping it right!" He squinted at the kerosene lamp burning brightly in the corner of the room. "Let's work extra-hard tomorrow and get all the hoeing done before sunset."

They sat around the evening fire for a while longer and talked small talk, but everyone was tired. Luami was the first one to lie down on her mat for the night, and soon Motumba followed. Little Abu was already asleep in Abena's arms. Tomorrow would be a busy day if they were going to get ready for their first Sabbath.

Chapter 6

"We are blessed with good children," Abena said as she glanced at her husband fondly. "I just wish we could give them a chance to really do something with their lives."

"We send them to school when we have the money," Danso replied. "That's a start, especially for Motumba. What else can we do?"

"I don't know." Abena had a faraway look in her eye. "We are Christians now, and I think we must do more."

"What do you have in mind?" Danso stared at his wife intently.

"I don't know for sure," she began, "but I've been thinking. For one thing, we need to find a church where we can worship, as Kossi's book tells us we must."

"I've been thinking the same thing," Danso replied. Many husbands might not discuss such things with their wives, but Danso valued his wife's opinion. Besides being a good mother and a hard worker, she was smart.

"And there's another thing," Abena added. "Motumba is growing into a man, and still we do not have a plan for his future."

"What would you like to see him do?"

"That is probably mostly up to him and you to decide. He is a very religious boy—maybe he would make a good pastor. We should ask him what he is interested in doing." Abena adjusted the wick in the kerosene lamp. Its tiny flickering flames made giant shadows jump and dance in animated shapes on the smooth clay wall. Abena wasn't used to challenging her husband on such important issues. Making decisions like this was a man's job.

"I've heard there are Christian secondary schools near the big cities," Danso finally said, "but I'm sure they're very expensive. We could never afford them."

"They say money is not always a problem." Abena was determined that this discussion would not die for lack of energy. "Kossi said lots of young men and even boys sell books and Bibles to earn a scholarship there."

"Maybe we could let him do that for a few years until he can earn enough. He could do that part-time while he helps on the farm."

"I don't think that's a good idea," Abena said adamantly. "He's 15 already. If he tries to sell books and work on the farm at the same time, he'll never get out of here. He'll be too tied to the farm."

"But I need him. We struggle now as it is, and with one less hand to help out, it will be impossible to get the work done."

"No, it won't," she dared to argue her point. "We are dependent on him, but we can get along without him. Grandpa is here and I can help more. Motumba needs to go to school now. There is so much he needs to learn. If we wait until college or university to send him for religious training, it will take him years to catch up. With all we've discovered in the Bible and the book Kossi sold us, we've only scratched the surface of the things God wants to show us. We're learning about baptism and the Sabbath and what really happens to people when they die."

She sighed as if the weight of the world were on her shoulders. "There's too much at stake here. I have this terrible feeling that time is going to get away from us, that Motumba will end up doing what we have done all our lives. I don't want that for him, do you?"

"No, you're right," Danso finally conceded. "He should go now."

"And Luami? She should have a chance at an education too," Abena said as she lifted her soft brown eyes to her husband. She was treading on dangerous ground, trying to do so much in one night, but for some reason she felt she must. Talk of education was important, and Luami had just as much at stake as Motumba.

"It's different for Luami," Danso replied confidently. "She's a girl."

"No, it's not different," Abena persisted. "We cannot think that just being a wife and having children will satisfy Luami. She is not interested in those things. Must we let her dry up and waste her life doing ordinary things simply because that is the way of our people?"

"Ordinary? I think ordinary is fine!" Danso's eyes flashed. "She must have a family someday, Abena. If not now, when? Would you have her go to university and become too good for the likes of us ordinary people?" He said the words almost sarcastically.

"Going to university will not make Luami too good for us. It will make her into a better person." Abena urged home her point. "In the end she will be 10 times the mother she is capable of being now."

"And what's wrong with her now? She's had six grades of primary education already." Danso was beginning to raise his voice.

"Nothing's wrong with her," Abena replied, glancing around at the sleeping children, "but Luami's already discontented with the things we're pushing her to do now."

"She's fine!" he said bluntly.

"It's the way it's done in many places in the world." Abena's arguments were losing steam, and her voice grew softer.

"Babban Zugu is not the world," Danso said as he set his jaw. "It's not necessary for Luami to have that much education. It's not the way of our people."

Abena gave up the argument for now. She had gained something for Motumba tonight, if not Luami. There would be opportunities to do more for Luami later.

All the next morning Danso, Motumba, and Grandfather Manu continued hoeing the beans in their field. They didn't have that much left to do—the plot of ground was only two hectares (five acres) in size, but they needed to finish. As Motumba had reminded them before, working among the plants much longer would risk the crop because the blossoms were beginning to appear on the plants. Now and then Grandpa Manu would frown and take a swipe at one of the large grasshoppers feeding on the bean plants. He said little, but Danso knew Grandpa was thinking about the plague of locusts that had come to the region when he was a boy.

They worked quickly under the shade of their pointed, wide-brimmed leather hats as the sun climbed its way into the sky now painted a chalky blue. The morning was hot and biting flies were torture to their bare legs, but they kept up their pace.

No one talked, not even about the new book they had bought from Kossi. Motumba tried to keep up with his father and grandfather, but he was less experienced with a hoe. At their speed he began to fall farther and farther behind.

About midmorning a group of Motumba's friends came by on the road. "Why don't you come to the river with us for a swim?" they called, waving their hands excitedly. Rivulets of dirty sweat ran down Motumba's neck and back. He wanted to go with them in the worst way, but he knew he couldn't. There was so much left to do in the bean field, and it wouldn't be right to leave his father and grandfather to do all the work. Play could wait. He must do his part.

"Nah, I've gotta work!" he shouted back at them. "We've got to get this field done by nightfall!" Motumba stared at the long unfinished rows, and then wistfully watched his friends go on their way before he turned back to his work.

Grandpa glanced at Motumba some 50 yards behind them and stopped to lean on his hoe. "He's a good boy, Danso. Not a lazy bone in his body. You should be proud of him."

"He is at that," Danso agreed, "but like he said, this field must be done before dark, so we can celebrate the Sabbath tomorrow. There'll be time enough for him to go with his friends next week."

Noon finally came, and they took a siesta break to get inside and escape the heat. No one felt like eating much as they lay on their mats cooling themselves with wide fans made from twisted strands of straw. When they finally went back to the field, the temperature was still high, but the sun was halfway across the western sky and less direct. It was a race against time now.

Fortunately the last few rows of beans were on the western side of the field, so they were able to work in the shade during the late hours of the day. And to their surprise the weeds seemed more sparse, so they all made better progress than they had hoped. When it became obvious they would finish the task before dark, they all began to relax a bit.

Finally Grandpa paused in his work again. "We've got only these two rows left now, Danso. Why don't you let the boy go for a swim? He deserves it, and you know he'd be grateful."

Chapter 7

Danso straightened up and wiped the sweat from his steaming brow. "You're right," he said, smiling wearily at his father and glancing across the field at the work they had accomplished. "You are kind to think of the boy."

"I was once a boy myself, and so were you," Grandpa Manu grinned.

"Motumba!" Danso called. "Finish that last row you're on and take the rest of the afternoon off. Find your friends and take a dip in the river if you'd like! You've done enough for today!"

Motumba straightened up in surprise like a blade of grass after a morning rain shower. "Thank you, Papa." He hurried down the row, finishing the last few plants in record time, and then scampered off to the river.

"Oh, to be young again" Grandpa sighed as he watched Motumba run. "Did we ever run like that, Danso? I'm having a hard time remembering."

Danso was surprised at the feeling it gave him to let the boy go, but he smiled too. "We did, Papa, and I daresay, if you were headed to the river to swim right now, you'd run too."

"Why don't we, then?" Grandpa winked at Danso. "I say we go as soon as we're finished here."

Danso grinned at his father. "All right, then, I'll race you to the end of the row." And with that the weeds began flying like jumping grasshoppers on a hot summer's day.

The men were tired after a long day in the fields, so the swim in the river was refreshing, but best of all was the relief to have the field of beans all weeded, as they had hoped. When the cool of the evening descended on the little farm, the men sat down to one of Abena's tasty meals of rice and fou-fou. And for a treat, they all had fish that Motumba had caught that afternoon at the river.

The evening sun was setting behind the long row of trees west of the house, and Danso had just asked God's blessing on the meal when Kossi suddenly showed up, to everyone's surprise.

"What a perfect ending to an already perfect day!" Danso exclaimed as everyone jumped up and crowded around the young book salesman. They invited him to sit down and eat with them. After a long day on the road, he was only too happy to accept.

"We've been reading that book you sold us, and it's already changed our lives so much!" Danso said with a smile. "We've read some surprising things about Bible prophecy, and the end of the world, and what happens to people when they die."

"And we found out that the seventh day of the week is the real rest day God wants Christians to worship on!" Luami said excitedly, forgetting that she was supposed to keep quiet when there were guests in the house. "This will be our very first Sabbath!"

Danso smiled at his daughter's enthusiasm, and so did Kossi. "It's all so new to us," Danso added, "but I wanted to ask you, How can this seventh-day Sabbath thing possibly be right? I know of no one who does such a thing."

"So you've discovered the Sabbath?" Kossi grinned from ear to ear. "That's a good one, but it's quite plain in the Bible, as I'm sure you can see. God created the world in six days and rested on the seventh. He asks that we celebrate its holiness with Him too. In fact, He commands that we do no work on that day, so that we can rest from all our labors."

Danso nodded. "It's interesting you should mention that. Just last night we decided we needed to keep our first Sabbath tomorrow, so we worked hard all day to finish hoeing the beans."

Kossi couldn't stop grinning. "Well, it looks as if God has provided you with time to get some real rest, then! What do you say we celebrate it together with God? In fact, according to the Bible, the Sabbath starts on Friday evening when the sun sets. The evening and the morning were the measurement of time when God first created the world, so that's when the Sabbath actually begins."

"So the Sabbath is beginning right now?"

"It is," Kossi nodded. "Would you like to pray with me right now to invite God into your home as it starts?"

"Of course." Danso bowed his head, and everyone followed his example as Kossi prayed. It was a simple prayer designed for this family who was discovering God's truth in all its glory. Danso and Abena had such a look of peace on their faces. In fact, the whole family felt different this night. Had Kossi made the difference, they all wondered, or was it something else? Was it maybe this idea of the Sabbath rest he talked about?

Night birds called out to one another as the darkness deepened outside. Abena lit the kerosene lamp, and Danso took *Bible Readings for the Home* down from its shelf on the wall. The list of questions Danso had for Kossi was almost endless. Grandpa Manu talked some too, but the children just sat and listened. As was the custom in West Africa, children were taught to listen when visitors came.

Abena listened quietly too. She was tired after her long day of work pounding maize in the wooden mortar, washing clothes on the rocks at the river, and making the rice and fou-fou they ate that night for supper. But she was intrigued by what was being said too, and her mind raced ahead of the discussion.

Finally she spoke. "I was wondering. How many people worship like this every Sabbath day?"

"You mean in this area?" Kossi smiled at the innocence of her question. "There's a church in Agwarra on the road to Bin Yauri. I think there are about 25 members coming regularly. That's the closest church group. It's maybe 50 kilometers [30 miles] away. They are Seventh-day Adventists, and they worship God on the Sabbath, as your book says. In fact, they come from the same church organization that published the book you're reading."

"Really?" Abena's eyes brightened. "There's a whole church of Sabbath worshippers, and they published our book?"

"Yes, well, actually the group is not even really a church yet. It's a company of believers, but they meet every Sabbath."

"A company? What's a company?"

"A company of believers is a group of worshippers who are too small to have a church building of their own, but they have a pastor who comes every other week. An old elder in the church preaches on the other Sabbaths, and I help sometimes too when I come this way."

"And they call themselves Seventh-day—what did you call them?"

"Seventh-day Adventists. Kind of a complicated name, isn't it?" Kossi almost laughed. "The country of Nigeria has many of these groups. Actually, there are more than 1,000 churches and companies at last count."

"And the closest church is 50 kilometers [30 miles] away? I wish we could go there sometime," Abena said wistfully.

"It's a long way to walk," Kossi nodded, "but we could do that, or if you can spare the money, you can catch a ride on a bus."

"We're short on money, but I really want to see how they worship." Abena glanced at Danso. "I'd be willing to walk."

"That's 50 kilometers [30 miles] each way," Kossi reminded her.

"Oh . . . that is quite a ways to walk." Abena frowned. "Maybe we could leave the children with friends. Luami and Abu would get too tired on that kind of trip. We can't expect them to walk that far."

"I want to go too!" Luami protested. "Don't leave me home!"

Abena glanced at Luami and then at Danso again. "Do you think the children could make it?"

"It would be nothing for Motumba," Danso said, grinning at his teenage son. "More like a holiday probably. And I think Luami could make it. It's Abu I'm worried about."

"I'll carry him strapped to my back like I always do," Abena said confidently. "How about next Sabbath? Can we afford to take some time off to make the trip?"

"The bean plants are starting to blossom, so it will be at least 10 days to two weeks before the first beans begin coming on. I think we could spare the time."

"Are you serious about walking?" Kossi looked a little worried.

"We can make it," Danso replied. "How about you, Papa?" he asked as he glanced at Manu. "Are you game?"

"I may be old, but I've got good legs," Grandpa Manu bragged.

"Then it's settled," Danso stated.

Kossi shook his head and grinned. "All right then, I'll meet you at the church on Sabbath. Here's the directions," he said as he scribbled notes on a piece of paper and handed it to Danso.

And so it was that the light of the gospel came to the house of Danso. Truth was shining where once there had been only the spiritual darkness of animism and spirit worship. And the angels struck a melodious chord and sang for joy at the new souls who had come one step closer to heaven.

Chapter 8

All the next week the family made plans for the trip to Agwarra. Walking 50 kilometers (30 miles) would be no simple task, but with the crop of beans not yet harvested, there was no money for them all to catch rides on a local bus.

The beans had had their final hoeing now, and the blossoms had appeared and then disappeared in just a few days as the small bean pods emerged from the blossoms. The family anxiously watched to see if the beans would fill out nicely. The weather was drier than usual, but the beans seemed to be doing OK. "I think it might be wise for us to carry water again from the well to give the plants just a little extra water," Danso told Motumba early one morning as they examined the plants.

Motumba's face fell a bit at this announcement, but Danso was quick to add, "We don't have to do it all in one day, son. But if we get up early in the morning and do a couple of rows before it gets hot, and then a few more rows just before dark, the job won't be so bad. That will give the plants a bit more of a boost, don't you think?"

Motumba shrugged. "It won't be so bad, I guess. And besides, we have the Agwarra trip to look forward to," he said with a grin.

Danso laughed. "That's the spirit, Motumba!" And father and son set about hauling buckets of water from the well at the back of the house to the field. By the time Thursday arrived, they had watered the entire field, one row at a time.

Late Thursday afternoon the family left on their trip to the city. With all the things they had to carry, they looked like a family of refugees, carrying enough food for at least five days, a large pot to cook in, several large skins of water, and a bundle of clean clothes for everyone. Danso knew he and Motumba could have made the trip in one day, but with the younger children along, he knew such a thing was impossible.

They made progress that afternoon and evening, and by the time they finally stopped to build a campfire and settle in for the night, they had gone quite a distance. "How far have we gone?" Abena asked with a heavy sigh as she put some rice into the pot Grandpa Manu had been carrying.

"About 15 or 16 kilometers [nine or 10 miles], as nearly as I can estimate.

I'm glad we decided to leave today instead of tomorrow." Danso squatted down beside the fire and put some green grass on the flames to discourage the mosquitoes from coming around. "We'll have a much easier time of it tomorrow for all the effort we've put in today."

They all lay down on their sleeping mats early that night in the field beside the road. The stars accented the deep indigo twilight sky, and then the big round moon rose in all its glory. As it began its journey into the heavens, it slowly changed from amber to saffron to pale-blue white. Crickets serenaded them from their snug hideouts among the bambusa bushes, and nighthawks chirped and whistled on their swooping rounds through the evening sky. But no one stayed awake long enough to enjoy any of it. In a matter of minutes everyone was asleep.

Early Friday morning before the sky had turned a violet pink, the family was up again. They ate a quick breakfast of maize kenkey, and then they were off again on their trip to the city. They wanted to get a good start before the day got too hot. During the first few hours it was cooler, and they traveled quickly. Luami did much better than everyone expected, and even Abu seemed to enjoy the trip, though he had to remain on Abena's back where he was tied with a long length of mud cloth.

They took a break near noon, and after a well-deserved siesta under an afara tree, they continued on their way. By the time they arrived in Agwarra late that afternoon, Abena looked exhausted, but she refused to complain. "I wouldn't miss this chance to see fellow believers like us for anything in the world," she exclaimed.

They found the Seventh-day Adventist church easy enough, and set up camp for the night. "I hope this is all right," Danso told his father. "We look a lot like squatters, with all the baggage we've brought."

Sabbath morning arrived bright and clear, and everyone was up at the crack of dawn. They bathed and dressed in their clean clothes, and then ate a hurried breakfast. Before long Kossi arrived. He greeted them with a smile and then introduced them all to Pastor Kwame and several members who had also come quite a distance.

Abena's eyes shone with anticipation as the members settled in for the morning Sabbath School. "This is our very first Sabbath in a real church," she whispered to Danso, who was all smiles as he took in their surroundings. They were enjoying a well-deserved rest. Not having to go to the fields to work, as they did every other day of the week, was a real treat. The children were wide-eyed with anticipation at everything they saw. It was all so new to them.

After a few minutes a man got up and led out in a brief song service. The songs were like nothing Danso and Abena had ever heard before, but they did their best to join in with the other members. Such songs as "Amazing Grace" filled their hearts with peace, and Abena especially liked the words to the song "A Shelter in the Time of Storm."

Then they all opened their Bibles to study the Word of God. The subject of the day was baptism, a topic the family had read about in Kossi's book. After a while a friendly woman who had a big smile came and asked the children if they wanted to go with her for some special activities for the young people. Abena was surprised when Abu agreed to go with Luami. Later the children told her all about the Bible story the teacher told, and the Picture Roll she used to illustrate it.

Pastor Kwame preached a stirring message on faithfulness to God in everything we do. He told them that faithfulness meant they should honor His Sabbath, share the good news of salvation with their neighbors, and pay their tithe as a way of giving back to God.

He read from Malachi 3 and challenged those who hadn't begun yet to join in the habit of paying tithe. Then he prayed for all the members gathered in the church and sent them on their way with God's blessing.

After church Danso and Abena were invited along with Kossi to go to the pastor's home to eat the noon meal. They enjoyed a wonderful meal of couscous, rice with beans, and a stew made from yams and guinea fowl eggs. To finish the meal, Pastor Kwame's wife gave them a special treat of fried plantains sweetened with sugarcane juice.

After the meal Pastor Kwame had a chance to get to know Danso and his family a bit better. They talked of many things—the farm, the crops, the weather. Pastor Kwame then told them about how the gospel message was going to all the world with the help of the radio. He turned his radio on at 3:00 that afternoon so they could hear a radio program called *The Voice of Prophecy.* There was beautiful music, and poems were recited, and a man with a deep voice spoke encouraging words from the Bible.

"I've been thinking of what you talked about in church today about tithing," Danso finally said. "We read some Bible verses about it in a book Kossi sold us. The book says we should pay 10 percent of 'our increase.' But we make very little on our farm. If we give 10 percent, we'll have even less. Does God really expect us to pay tithe when we're poor?"

"He does," Pastor Kwame said, nodding solemnly. "He gives us so much, and tithing is just one way for us to say thank You for His blessings. In fact, the verses we read today at church challenge us to test God. Let's read it again. It's in Malachi, chapter 3, verses 10 and 11." Pastor Kwame and Kossi found the spot and held their Bibles so Danso and Grandpa Manu could read along too.

" ' "Bring all the tithes into the storehouse, that there may be food in My house, and try Me now in this," says the Lord of hosts, "if I will not open for you the windows of heaven and pour out for you such blessing that there will not be room enough to receive it. And I will rebuke the devourer for your sakes, so that he will not destroy the fruit of your ground, nor shall the vine fail to bear fruit for you in the field," says the Lord of hosts.' "

"That sounds pretty clear, doesn't it?" Pastor Kwame looked up from his Bible. "God sends the rain and sunshine to make your crops grow. He's given you a wonderful wife, smart, healthy children, and a happy home. He even brought the good news of the gospel to your door. Don't you think paying anything less than a full 10 percent of your increase would be an insult to Him?"

"It seems so," Danso said quietly. He shrugged and glanced at Abena. "I guess there's no question about what we should do, then. When our crop is sold, we must set aside one tenth of the money we get. Who shall we give it to?"

"You can bring it to the church here, if you like." Pastor Kwame nodded matter-of-factly. "The money is used to support the ministry and spread the gospel so Jesus can come again soon."

"That's good enough for me," Grandpa Manu exclaimed. "If it supports projects such as Kossi selling his good books, I'm for it."

"Are we supposed to pay tithe only at harvesttime?" Motumba asked. He had been quiet all during the discussion, but now he spoke up, and his insight impressed the preacher.

"Well, that depends on your circumstances," Pastor Kwame said. "Some people pay once a week or once a month, depending on when they get paid for work. Some pay their tithe when they are given money for something they sell, or when the crops come in."

"If we have money right now that we haven't paid tithe on, should we do that?"

Pastor Kwame smiled at this mature lad who was already way ahead of the game. Instead of trying to do the least he possibly could in fulfilling one of God's requirements, it appeared he was thinking they should go the extra mile. "Motumba, that is exactly what God would have you do," he said reverently, "and I'm glad you see things that way. God has a place in His work for young men who will look for chances to honor Him and His church."

Motumba bowed his head respectfully at these kind words, but Danso and Abena glanced at each other perceptively. Maybe their dreams for Motumba's schooling would have a chance after all.

Chapter 9

Danso paid his very first tithe in answer to Pastor Kwame's challenge. It was a test of faith to be sure. Danso had brought only 750 naira with him on the trip, and to part with 75 naira's worth of hard-earned coins seemed a stretch for his faith. "God will bless you far and above what you think you may be giving up now," Pastor Kwame assured him. "You can't outgive the Lord."

The Sabbath ended a few hours later in a blaze of glory as the golden sun quickly dipped behind the horizon to the west. They sang a hymn, and then listened as Pastor Kwame repeated a portion of Psalm 19, one of his favorite chapters from David's songs. "'The heavens declare the glory of God; the skies proclaim the work of his hands. . . . In the heavens he has pitched a tent for the sun, which is like a bridegroom coming out of his chamber, like a champion rejoicing to run his course. It rises at one end of the heavens and makes its circuit to the other; nothing is deprived of its warmth'" (verses 1-6, TNIV).

They all retired early that night. Morning would come all too soon. The trip home the next day would be long, and they needed their rest. As they fell asleep under the stars again, they knew the journey had been successful. They had met with like believers, and they had enjoyed the sweet fellowship that comes with worshipping in God's house. They had also discovered the truth about tithing. It was a new idea to them, but they had no way of knowing just how much of an impact it was going to have on their lives.

The trip home was uneventful. The weather was cooler, thanks to some cloud cover, and it even rained during the late afternoon. Everyone grew weary by the end of the day, and when the family stopped short of home just after sunset, Luami and Abu fell asleep without even eating. Grandpa Manu built a fire, and Abena heated up some rice. Everyone ate quickly, because they were all eager to lie down on their sleeping mats.

"It was good to visit the church in Agwarra," Danso said wearily, "but I'll be glad to get back home." Everyone agreed. Even Abena.

By midmorning the next day they were home again. Little Abu was overjoyed to be in familiar surroundings again, and he ran around and around the house, shouting excitedly. Luami soon resumed her favorite game—catching frogs and worms and grasshoppers. Abena had to call her several times impatiently to help around the house.

"I was looking for Goliath," Luami protested. "He got away!"

"Well, I can't say I'm sorry," Abena retorted. "You spend too much time fussing with that bug."

"It's not a bug. It's a grasshopper," Luami argued.

"Actually, it's a locust," Motumba said as he stepped inside to get a drink of water.

"A locust?"

"Yup. They're usually bigger than grasshoppers," he said between gulps of cool water. "The ones in our fields are brown-looking, and they fly as much as they jump."

Luami's eyes were wide as her brother continued talking about the locust grasshoppers. She admired Motumba in many ways. He was the smartest boy around, and he treated her kindly. To her, he was the best brother any African girl could have!

The bean field was doing nicely now. During the next few days Motumba and the men watered the plants one more time, tenderly caring for their crop. Everyone was getting excited. In a matter of days they would begin harvesting the beans, which were growing quite large on the vine, to sell in the markets. The beans could be picked green, or they could be allowed to dry on the vines before being picked and shelled.

That evening the family gathered at the front of the house to tell stories. A fire was lit as the moon came up, and Luami and Abena sang some folk songs to entertain the family. Father and Grandfather talked about politics and the old colonial days when their country was run by the British. While the adults talked, little Abu found a grasshopper in the dark and brought it to his father and set it in his lap.

"This is strange," Danso laughed. "Mr. Grasshopper isn't even trying to get away. Maybe he's cold."

"I think it's because he can't see," Motumba stated. "I read in school that grasshoppers have hundreds of eyes, and they all reflect light. So at night they can't see. That's why he's not moving much."

"And maybe he's afraid of the fire, too," Grandpa Manu said as he leaned forward and threw another stick of wood on the evening fire. The flames immediately began licking at the new timber.

"It looks as if we're more afraid of him than he is of us." Danso frowned as he stared down at the grasshopper. "When we came through town this morning, I heard some talk that the locusts are multiplying in greater numbers to the north. I hope they don't come farther south. That could mean disaster for all the farmers in the area."

"I hope so too," Grandpa chimed in. "A plague of locusts is the worst thing one can possibly imagine this time of year. War is bad and disease can be devastating, but grasshoppers are the scourge of northern Nigeria." He shivered even as the flames of the fire warmed the family. "If they grow too large in number and become a grasshopper plague, they could eat every green thing in sight," and with that he launched into one of his lengthy explanations of what exactly a plague of locusts can do.

"Tell us a story," Motumba offered, hoping to distract Grandpa Manu enough to tell them a story they hadn't heard in a long time.

"So, you want a story?" the old man asked. His eyes squinted as if he were deep in thought. "All right, I've got just the one. I've been reading some of the questions in that book Mr. Kossi sold us, and then I got out the Bible to read some texts, and wouldn't you know it, I found a really good story. You'll never guess what it's about."

Motumba's eyes grew bright in anticipation. "Let me guess, grass-hoppers?"

"That's exactly it!" Grandpa smiled a toothy grin in the flickering firelight. He paused and stared into the dancing flames for the longest while, and then he began the tale slowly and deliberately. "This story happened a long, long time ago when the earth was young. God's people had been slaves since forever it seemed, and now God was delivering them from the clutches of the mighty Pharaoh of Egypt.

"God was punishing Pharaoh for not setting His people free. He turned the river to blood, sent frogs to cover the land, and even caused disease and hail to fall on their cattle. But still that stubborn, old king would not listen to common sense. He would not obey God, so God sent another plague, and this time it was locusts, or grasshoppers as we often call them.

"When the grasshoppers descended on Egypt, the sky grew dark and ominous! They made a hissing sound that roared as if a howling sandstorm were drawing closer. The locusts landed on the grass and bushes and trees along the roads. They landed on the ripening fields of flax and barley that had been beaten to the ground by a hailstorm only a few days before that. Worse still, the grasshoppers landed on the green fields of wheat and lentils that were still partly standing.

"It didn't seem to matter if a plant was growing or dead, green or dry—the old locusts ate everything in sight. They weighed down the grass and totally covered the palm trees."

Everybody around the fire shuddered as they listened to the story. They had heard Grandpa tell his stories about grasshoppers, but they had never seen such a horrible sight with their own eyes. Luami and Motumba were totally transfixed by the story. Their mouths hung open, and their eyes were big with wonder. Grandpa was one of the best storytellers around, so things came to life when he talked, and this story was no exception. He was really outdoing himself this time.

Chapter 10

"The swarming locust hordes looked like a big army of creeping, crawling creatures," Grandpa continued. "The ground in Egypt was alive with the grasshoppers, and everyone ran here and there to get away from them. But they couldn't escape. The locusts crawled into their clothes and hair. Their prickly little legs scratched their skin and drove everyone crazy! There were just too many of them! Even the wells began to fill up with the squirming, crawling insects, making it impossible to get a drink of fresh water!

"But God's people were protected from the locusts. It was incredible! Not one grasshopper came to the land of Goshen where the Israelites lived! God took care of His people, and none of their crops were eaten! It was a miracle!"

"Did the Bible really say all that?" Luami asked, her eyes still big.

"Well, I did add a few details, but then again, I've been through a plague of locusts before, so you can't really blame me now, can you, child?"

"And that's the end of the story," Abena said sleepily as she yawned and picked up Abu where he was sleeping on a grass mat. "It's time we all went to sleep. The beans will be ready to pick in just a few days, so we'd better rest while we can."

The next morning dawned bright and clear, and it promised to be another hot one. No rain had fallen for more than three weeks now. Fortunately, there had been a little dew some nights, but even so the leaves on the bean vines were beginning to wilt under the intense heat of the African sun.

"This is bad news for the crop," Danso said when he came in from the field before breakfast. "The beans need water badly."

"The beans that are almost ready to pick will be all right," Grandpa Manu said. He stood up and surveyed the field. "But the second round to be picked will definitely be skimpy if we don't get any rain."

Abena set a pot of rice on the table with some sour kenkey, and then she went to wake Luami. Motumba, yawning and stretching, came to the table with his shirt still off. Abu was already up and trying to feed the cat some of Abena's kenkey. His little voice could be heard instructing the cat in no uncertain terms that he must eat the kenkey. Unfortunately, the cat didn't like the idea of being force-fed, and much less sour kenkey at that.

"Before we start the day, let's read a scripture for morning worship like Kossi has taught us to do," Danso said, opening the family Bible. "Here's the one I marked in my Bible when we were at Pastor Kwame's house. "'Bring all the tithes into the storehouse, that there may be food in My house, and try Me now in this," says the Lord of hosts, "If I will not open for you the windows of heaven and pour out for you such blessing that there will not be room enough to receive it. And I will rebuke the devourer for your sakes, so that he will not destroy the fruit of your ground, nor shall the vine fail to bear fruit for you in the field," says the Lord of hosts.' That's in Malachi 3:10 and 11," Danso added.

"What's a devourer, Papa?" Luami asked, rubbing the sleep from her eyes.

Danso smiled at his daughter's serious face. "A devourer is something that eats everything."

Luami had such a serious look on her face, but she never missed a beat. "Like Motumba when he eats Mama's food?" Everyone laughed at that comment, and even Motumba had to smile.

"No, Luami, I wouldn't worry too much about Motumba. He's still growing, but we are a bit worried about some of the things that can eat up our gardens."

"Like grasshoppers?" Luami came over and sat down on Danso's lap. She still liked being her papa's little girl.

"Like grasshoppers," Danso agreed, putting his arms around her. "They can destroy all that we've worked so hard to grow. They can invade our fields and eat our bean plants down to the ground in no time at all." He glanced down at the open Bible on the table. "I guess people in the Bible had trouble with insects that could eat their crops too. That must be what the writer meant."

"So will God help us and keep the grasshoppers from de-vo-ur-ing our beans?" Luami pronounced the difficult word slowly.

"I hope so," Danso shrugged. "If we are faithful to pay our tithes, the Bible says it will be so."

Luami looked at her papa solemnly. "You don't really believe God will do that for us, do you, Papa?"

There was a painful silence as Danso hesitated a bit and hung his head. "I think He can," he finally replied.

Abena nodded. "Don't forget, Papa, that God has promised He will provide everything we need, no matter what. The birds and flowers don't worry about what they need to survive. Why should we? God says all things will work together for the good of those who love Him. Remember those texts we read in our book?"

"You're right, Mama," Danso sighed. "We must trust that God will care for us and our bean crop."

"Even if it means that God lets His grasshoppers eat up our beans?" Motumba suddenly added, a smile playing around the corners of his mouth.

Danso hesitated only a moment. "Even if—the grasshoppers eat up our beans."

The room was quiet for a few moments longer as everyone sat thinking of what that might mean.

"I wish my family had had that kind of faith when I was a boy and the grasshopper plague came," Grandpa Manu said quietly.

"What did you do?" Luami slid off Danso's lap and went to stand by Grandpa Manu.

"We fell apart. All of us. Everybody in the village was devastated, and no one knew what to do."

Luami's eyes grew sad. "What did you do then?"

"Nothing. There was nothing we could do. All our crops were gone, eaten down to the ground. It was the hardest of times for my father and mother."

"You could have prayed."

"My father didn't know how to pray. We weren't Christians. We didn't know about the Bible promises of God's protection and care. We didn't know Jesus, and my father didn't think being a Christian was important for our family. We worshipped the spirits."

"And you didn't know about paying tithe?"

"No, we knew nothing of that. I think only Christians know about tithe."

A great stillness filled the room once again. "I thank God that we know of Jesus and the help He can give us," Danso finally said. "Let us pray." They all bowed their heads reverently, and Danso began talking to his new Friend: "Lord, we are grateful for everything that comes from above. We thank You for bringing Kossi to us and the good books that have showed us Your truth. Bless our bean field, Lord. We have paid our tithe, and we claim Your promise that You will protect us from the devourer. Those pesky grasshoppers can destroy everything, Lord. We pray especially that You will keep them away from eating our beans. In Jesus' name we pray our prayer, as Kossi has taught us. Amen."

"And now it's time we all got to work. Motumba, I've got good news and bad news. Which do you want to hear first?"

Motumba frowned. "The good news, 'cause I think I already know what the bad news is."

"All right, the good news is that the beans are coming along nicely. I was out early this morning, and the first crop seems to be doing well. The clay in the soil has kept the moisture below ground for the plants."

Motumba half smiled. "And the bad news?"

"The bad news is I want to water the plants at least one more time."

Motumba groaned.

"It could mean the difference between a good crop and a poor one."

Motumba looked unconvinced and unimpressed.

"Well now, the day is young!" Grandpa Manu announced. "If we get out and do plenty now, we can rest during the hottest parts of the day. Maybe you can even take a swim in the river with your friends during our break, Motumba. But first we must work!"

Chapter 11

Motumba, Danso, and Grandpa Manu went outside. Little puffs of dust swirled around their feet and then rose up on the early-morning air. "It sure is dry out," Danso said, squinting up at the morning sky, "but the wind is picking up and the sky has an eerie look about it. Maybe we'll get some rain and we won't have to water the beans after all." He threw his arm across his son's shoulder. "It's not rained this early in the day for a long time."

Abena came to stand by her husband. She, too, glanced at the darkening sky. "It does look strange, doesn't it?" she frowned. "Is that the wind I hear?"

"Doesn't sound much like wind to me," Motumba said. By this time the rest of the family was out in the yard staring at the sky.

"What do you make of it, Grandpa?" Danso turned to his father as the rising wind ruffled the leaves on the trees in the yard. "It sounds more like hissing than anything else. Is that really the wind?"

Grandpa Manu had a strange look in his eyes as he took off his pointed leather hat. "That's not a storm coming!" he almost shouted. "It's a swarm of locusts!"

"A swarm of locusts!" Danso turned to his father in alarm. "You're kidding!"

"I wouldn't kid about a thing like this, son! I'd recognize that sound anywhere! See that swirling moving mass of gray over there on the horizon?" He pointed to the north. "They're coming all right! I'd say we have about five minutes before they hit us full force! Maybe 10 at the most!"

"Ten minutes!" Panic gripped Danso like nothing he had ever experienced before. "What'll we do!"

"There's nothing we can do except pray!" Grandpa dropped to his knees. Abena fell to her knees too, but Danso refused to give in. He stood staring at the sky, a feeling of hopelessness sweeping over him. "There must be something we can do!" he stammered. "Anything! We can't just stand here and let them come! They'll destroy the bean crop we've worked so hard to raise! They'll take everything!" His voice rose to an angry crescendo.

But Grandpa was praying and didn't answer. Abena was on her knees in the dust, and Danso could hear her reciting some Bible verses. "'He who dwells in the secret place of the Most High shall abide under the shadow of the Almighty'" (Ps. 91:1). Her voice was soon overpowered by the whirring wind of locusts coming their way, but on she prayed. During the previous weeks she had come to love the family Bible, and had committed to memory many favorite verses of Scripture. Whether she was pounding corn in the wooden mortar, or washing clothes, or hoeing in the family garden, the Bible had come to be her comfort and joy, and now these verses were her strength.

"There's millions of 'em!" Motumba shouted above the whir of locust wings. "Look at 'em!" A strange light came into Motumba's eyes as he watched them come. Unfortunately, he was too young and too naïve to imagine the devastation that was about to hit the farm. Luami, however, sensed the seriousness of the moment, and like her father, her eyes widened with fear. She clutched little Abu's hand—he appeared unafraid as he pointed at the sky with his pudgy hand, his curious little eyes watching the coming "storm."

By now other neighbors had come out to look at the sky, and they began to panic and shout as they pointed at the approaching swarms. Their screams rose on the wind like the eerie wailing of mourners at a funeral for the dead.

Danso stood transfixed as the swirling mass of gray drew nearer and nearer in the darkening sky. "All will be lost!" he moaned as the whirring sound increased to a dull hiss on the morning air. His eyes darted this way and that as he tried to think of what he could do. "We've got to do something! They'll devour everything!" he kept saying as he lifted his hands helplessly to the sky! "The entire crop will be lost!"

The insects kept coming on their destructive path, but above the hiss of a billion beating wings, Abena's voice could still be heard. "The Lord's our Rock, in Him we hide, a shelter in the time of storm!" Her quavering voice sang the song they had learned just that week at church. "Secure whatever ill betide, a shelter in the time of storm."

And then the grasshoppers were upon them like a cloud of noxious vapor! They filled the hot morning air, swirling and spinning across the landscape as if trying to decide which way to turn! It was a terrifying sight!

Their clicking wings kept them hovering for a moment longer, and then they suddenly dropped to the fields! They covered the trees along the fields, weighing down the limbs until the branches touched the ground!

They swarmed everywhere upon the neighboring fields of corn and tomatoes and spinach! As they hit Danso's bean field, they covered it like a heavy blanket, flattening the stout bean vines to the ground! Wasting no time, they set to work with their mandibles, stripping the leaves from the plants, eating the ripe beans and the beans not yet ready to pick! They even chewed on the wiry stems of the bean vines! It was a sickening sight, and it was all happening just as Grandpa had described in his stories!

The army of creeping, crawling creatures moved across the field like a giant eating machine! Even the munching, crunching of their tiny jaws could be heard as they devoured the bean field that had come so close to being harvested!

"They're eating everything!" Luami screamed hysterically and ran to her mother for comfort. Abena was still on her knees, but she pulled her daughter close as they watched the hordes of insects ravage their bean field. "God has promised us that He will be with us," she shouted in Luami's ear. "He will not forsake us! We must depend on His goodness!" Abena was frightened too, but so far she had managed to remain calm, her steady voice not revealing the shell-shocked feeling of despair that threatened to sweep over her.

And then Danso suddenly roused himself to action. "We've got to stop them!" he shouted again. "Come on, Motumba! There may be millions of them, but no one is going to say we didn't try!" He raced off to the shed where they kept all their tools!

The two of them emerged a few moments later with hoes and rakes and shovels! Danso darted into the bean field now covered with a carpet of seething, moving grasshoppers! Their small bodies crunched under his feet as he ran, but he paid them no mind! With a hoe in each hand, he began swinging great arching swaths, taking out bean plants and hordes of grasshoppers as he ran. Motumba followed his example with two shovels, sending plants and dirt flying too!

"Come on, Papa!" Danso shouted at Grandpa Manu. "Grab a shovel or rake! We've got to scare them off!"

"It's no use," Grandpa called after him. "You can't stop them! There are too many of them!"

"We can do this!" Danso bellowed as he continued swinging the hoe with mighty blows that seemed to shake the ground. "If we all help, it'll make a difference!"

"No, you can't, son," Grandpa Manu called above the dull hiss of the locust plague. "I've seen this all before, and like it or not, they will march through our field and eat everything in sight. You can't stop them! You can't make a dent in them! You can kill thousands, but millions more will come to replace them! Only God can stop them now!"

It was hard to hear Grandpa talk like that. As if maybe God didn't really care about their plight. After all, if God wanted, He could stop the hordes of grasshoppers, couldn't He? He could prevent them from eating up the fields, could He not?

But that was the mystery of it all! God was not stopping the grasshoppers! He could, but He wasn't, and it pained Grandpa to think that maybe the family's newfound faith had all been a sham. He had worked as hard as anybody to get this crop ready for harvest, and now it seemed God had abandoned them in their time of greatest need. He was not protecting the field from the devourer as He had promised! The old man hung his head. Surely all was lost. His face showed the agony of having to surrender to the grasshoppers once again, the greatest enemy he had ever known.

Danso and Motumba beat at the relentless hordes with their tools for a few frenzied minutes, but the ravenous little beasts took no notice! The ferocious onslaught of tools and muscle seemed no more effective in their hands than if they had been trying to stop a herd of elephants! They worked at a maddening pace, cutting wide paths through the bean field, taking out hundreds of plants and thousands of insects in their wake! But a fresh wave of grasshoppers always fell in behind them, continuing on where the others had left off.

Chapter 12

Eventually Danso and Motumba began to tire. They slowed in their efforts, swinging their tools with less and less force until they finally stopped, their hoes and shovels hanging limp at their sides. Grandpa was right. There was nothing they could do but watch the horrible tragedy unfold!

The neighbors all up and down the road were out in their fields too. Some had followed Danso's example and tried to beat back the grasshoppers that had descended on their fields, but they had finally given up too. It was no use, and their pitiful wailing and screaming reached a new level as they all realized there was no hope for their crops. There was no doubt now that the grasshoppers would eat everything!

Danso's shoulders slumped as the locusts continued their rampage across the bean field. The patch was small, as bean fields go. Only two hectares (five acres) in size, and the insects were making short work of the beans. "We're ruined! All our hard work is gone now," he moaned. "The Lord has given, and the Lord has taken away!"

"I thought God would protect our fields if we paid our tithe," Motumba stammered. He was out of breath from the battle, and his young chest rose and fell from fatigue. "Why isn't He saving our fields?"

"I don't know, son!" Danso stammered in despair as he watched the locusts feasting on their beans, oblivious to the humans who had become mere spectators at the edge of the field.

Luami pulled at Danso's arm. "We've got to do something, Papa!" she wailed. "There must be something we can do!"

"There's nothing we can do." He repeated Grandpa's words of resignation. "Nothing at all!"

It saddened Abena to hear Danso's voice so full of despair. This was her husband, the one who desired more than anything to care for her and provide for the family. Now he was standing helpless before the hordes of devourers that had come to destroy everything their family had worked so hard to produce!

And then an idea struck Abena like an epiphany out of the blue. Must they indeed stand by and let these monsters of the northern desert come sweeping in to reap the rewards for which they had worked so long and so hard? Shouldn't humans be the ones in control here? After all, weren't humans superior to every other creature on earth, created in the image of God? The thought of all those pesky insects eating up their hard work made her just a little bit angry, and in that moment a sudden thought pushed its way into her mind.

Without a word, she rushed off to the shed, the deafening hiss of grasshoppers still loud in her ears. Before long she was back with a load of burlap sacks in each arm. "Danso! Motumba! Help me!" she called above the grasshopper storm. "Grab a sack!"

"What are these for?" Danso looked at Abena in surprise.

"Fill the sacks with grasshoppers!" Abena shouted excitedly as she rushed from Danso, to Motumba, to Grandpa. "Luami! You keep Abu out of the field!"

"Fill the sacks?" Danso retorted, confusion written on his tired, dirt-streaked face. "With grasshoppers? Why? The beans are nearly all gone! What's the point! You and Grandpa said so yourself!" He turned to stare at the field. "Look at the bean plants! The grasshoppers are covering them like glue! There's too many of them! The plants are finished! We can't win!"

And it was true. By now the grasshoppers had nearly eaten every green thing in sight. Long gone were the tender bean plants and pods, and still the grasshoppers managed to find something to chew on. But Abena seemed unaffected by her husband's arguments as she ran out into the bean patch, which was now totally decimated. Only scraggly stems of twisted bean vines remained behind as mute witnesses to the destruction of the advancing army.

"Help me catch the grasshoppers, everybody! Put them in the sacks!" she called, her voice fading as she ran down the rows of what had once been healthy bean plants.

Danso looked at Motumba, and Motumba stared right back. "What's she doing?" Danso asked impatiently, swatting at a grasshopper that whirred past his head.

"I have no idea!" Motumba shrugged, his face showing the same level of confusion. "Maybe she's trying to save what's left of the beans! It won't do any good! Any beans left are ruined anyway!"

"She wants us to help her catch the grasshoppers!" Luami shouted as she grabbed her father by the hand.

Danso glanced at Luami in surprise as if he had heard the command for the first time. "Catch the grasshoppers?" he asked. He turned and stared out across the field, a question mark on his face. *Is that what Abena is doing?* For a moment he forgot the devastation of the grasshopper plague as he thought of Luami's words. *Abena catching grasshoppers? But why?* "What're you doing?" he called again to Abena as he hurried out into the field.

By now she was scooping up big handfuls of the wriggling, crawling insects and stuffing them into the sacks. "I'm filling these sacks with grasshoppers, and if you're smart, you'll help too!" she said excitedly, her face flushed and already dripping with sweat as she continued on down the row. Grasshoppers were jumping up on her arms and neck and face, but she clawed at them and shoved them in the sack along with the others.

"You want us to help catch grasshoppers?" Danso called after her in exasperation as he pulled more of the gangling prickly bodies of grasshoppers from his hair and ears. "What for? We can't stop them! It's too late! The fields are destroyed!" Viciously he swatted at the pesky insects now biting him for lack of something else to eat. Why they were sticking around, he couldn't say. The field of green was all gone. Surely some instinctual drive was keeping them on his farm, but it wasn't the remaining foliage. There wasn't any. Even the leaves on the trees at the edge of the field were gone. Not one remained to shake and shimmer in the hot morning breeze. And still the grasshoppers stayed.

Abena stopped momentarily and turned around to stare at her husband. The weary, work-worn expression on Danso's face clearly showed a man who had been beaten. Gone was the drive to work hard. Gone was the bean crop he had worked hundreds of hours to produce. Gone was his faith in God.

"God has provided a way for us after all," Abena exclaimed. "He has blessed us with something we could've never expected, and we need to take advantage of it. We no longer have beans, Danso, but we have grasshoppers, and we can sell them in the market! People will buy them to eat!" She turned again to her work, calling over her shoulder as she ran. "Just fill the sacks, Danso! We're almost out of time! If we wait much longer the grasshoppers will all leave!"

Motumba and Grandpa Manu were in the field with Danso now, following along behind. "What does she want with the grasshoppers?" Motumba asked in frustration as dozens of grasshoppers jumped onto his shoulders and head, clinging to him. "Is she out of her mind!" he yelled as he fought the grasshoppers off violently—his patience at an end.

"Maybe." For a moment longer Danso watched his wife half walk, half run, stooping to the ground, her sack trailing along behind her as she worked feverishly. Motumba glanced at Grandpa Manu, but Grandpa only shrugged, wondering if Danso might be losing his mind too.

But a spark of life had now ignited itself in Danso, and the man wondered why it had taken so long for Abena's idea to register in his mind. Maybe all was not lost. Maybe there was a ray of hope in this disaster after all. "I think your mother may have something here." He squinted at the lone figure of his wife in the field. "Let's do as she says!" Without another word he ran to pick up his sack. Motumba followed along shaking his head, but he snatched up his sack and followed Danso's example.

"Strangest thing I ever did see," Grandpa Manu half-grumbled as he too headed out into the field. "Picking grasshoppers as if they were berries." But he was soon working as if someone had lit a fire under him.

"Come and help, Luami!" Abena yelled as she tied off one of her sacks and started filling another. "Grab a sack! I've already got one filled!"

"Eeek!" Luami screeched as she tried to pick up the squirmy, wriggling grasshoppers in her hand, but she soon got used to the sensation. She had enjoyed having Goliath as a pet, but this was different!

Chapter 13

The family hurried through the field of leafless, scraggly vines still swarming with the voracious eaters. Everyone was filling the sacks now with great handfuls of the huge insects, difficult though it seemed to be. It was the strangest sensation to grab up the squirming insects and push them into the sacks already bulging with the wriggling, creeping creatures. Danso set his mind to the task, clutching at the crawling, jumping locusts. Some tried to bite his hands and wrists, but he brushed them off as he plunged his hand into his sack again and again.

Motumba followed the family's example reluctantly, but his heart was not in it. "Chasing grasshoppers around the field as if they were toys is foolishness!" he muttered to himself as he kicked at the grasshoppers jumping up on his legs. "It's embarrassing! Craziest thing we've ever done!"

But Luami paid no mind to her brother, and set right to work doing her part. Soon she discovered that if she ran along dragging the open mouth of the sack on the ground, she could scoop up the grasshoppers even faster than the grown-ups. In no time at all she had two sacks of her own filled.

The work was tiring, but the family seemed to get a second wind, and worked faster and more furiously now to capture the swarming insects. Abena had inspired them all, and though they had no clear concept as to where this would all lead, they worked hard to fill their sacks with grasshoppers. They were a team. It had taken them time to catch on to Abena's idea, but once they started, like the grasshoppers, they moved across the field like a machine.

For more than an hour they worked to fill their sacks with the wriggling locusts. Everyone's back ached and their arms grew sore, but they kept on going. "Hurry!" Abena kept urging them. "We haven't much more time! Pray that God will keep the grasshoppers a little bit longer!"

Danso worked quickly beside his wife, and he had to wonder now at the strangeness of the moment. When the grasshoppers had first arrived, they had all prayed that God would rebuke the devourer. Now they were almost hoping God would keep the grasshoppers around a little longer.

How very strange are the providences of God! thought Danso as he scooped up huge handfuls of the insects.

And then Danso felt a change in the air. It was as if the frenzied munching of the scavenging insects had stopped, as if the crawling carpet of grasshoppers with one accord suddenly grew still. Danso's family stopped their work of gathering grasshoppers too, sensing that something was about to happen.

And then it did. Suddenly, as if by some mysterious signal sent forth from their commanding army general, the whole locust swarm rose on the southerly wind. The synchronized parts of the giant mowing machine all sailed off on the morning air just as quickly as they had come.

It was amazing! Within just a few minutes, there wasn't a grasshopper left. The bean field was now totally empty of plants and grasshoppers. All that remained were a few spindly bean stems that had proven themselves too tough even for the grasshopper hordes. The plants now looked for all the world like little stickmen standing guard in the wide-open, barren field. If it hadn't been such a serious thing, it might have looked comical. Not a leaf could be seen anywhere in the nearby forest of trees either. The locusts had chewed every green thing in sight, making the foliage disappear as if by magic.

The plague of locusts had been a terrifying sight, and as the family stared out across the stubble that had once been a field of flourishing bean plants, they knew hard times were ahead.

"Are they gone for good?" Luami finally broke the silence. "I never want to touch another grasshopper in my life! Not even Goliath!"

And then suddenly everybody started talking at once. "It's so quiet!" Motumba exclaimed in awe. "Kind of eerie-like!"

Grandpa started talking about how this grasshopper plague compared to the one he had experienced as a young boy, but Abena praised God. "Thank the Lord it's over!" she said again and again.

But Danso continued staring at the open field, a mixture of confusion and disbelief on his face. The immensity of destruction was beyond anything he had ever experienced. "I would like to know now," he finally stammered, as though he had woken up from a dream, "what on earth we are going to do with so many grasshoppers?"

"Well, first of all we need to praise the Lord for the good times and the bad," Abena said as she tied off her last sack of squirming insects and threw it onto the pile of bulging bags. "From everything Kossi and Pastor Kwame have told us, God has promised He will never abandon us."

"But He has abandoned us!" Motumba protested. "Look at our fields!" He pointed with a sweeping gesture at the bean field now stripped naked of all its foliage. "We have no beans! We'll have no money! What are we gonna do? The pastor told us if we paid our tithe God would rebuke the devourer! Well, they weren't rebuked! In fact, if anyone's been rebuked, it's us!"

"Motumba, don't be so hard on your mother," Grandpa Manu said, as he laid a hand on the young man's shoulder. "She's just trying to be brave and keep up our spirits."

"Well, I don't get it!" Motumba was in one of those rare moments when he seemed to forget his place. "We paid our tithe! Where was God? How come He didn't protect our bean fields like the Bible said He would?"

"You're right," Abena admitted. "God didn't protect our beans. In fact, He let the grasshoppers eat every last one of them!" Motumba stared at his mother, not sure where this was going. "But He did do something else for us," she added, "something none of us really expected. He gave us lots and lots of grasshoppers. Just look at them!" She pointed at the pile of trembling sackfuls of worming, squirming creatures trying to get out. "How many sackfuls of grasshoppers did we get?"

"I don't know." Motumba stared at the sacks, not giving his mother a chance to make her point. "Ten? Twenty? A hundred? Does it matter? Millions of grasshoppers eat up our beans, and you want to catch them instead of kill them? I don't get it! What's the point?"

Danso ignored Motumba's anger. "Well, let's see, I count . . . 1, 2, 3, 4, 5, 6, 7, . . . 14, 15, 16, . . . h'mmm, we have . . . 23 sacks of grasshoppers."

"And what are we going to do with them?" Motumba kept on with his tirade. "Kill them?"

Abena smiled tiredly at her eldest son. "Well now, Motumba, we could kill the grasshoppers. That's an idea, but I think we'd be better off taking them to town and letting our neighbors have them to eat."

"What!" Motumba looked as if he thought his mother was losing her mind for sure. "Are you kidding? If we do that, we're likely to get a good beating! The last thing the people in town want to see now is more grasshoppers! They've had enough of the pesky insects to last them a lifetime!"

"Are you sure about that?" Abena said with a touch of irony in her voice.

Danso finally cracked a smile, and then began to laugh at the look in Motumba's eye. Dirt streaks traced the rivulets of sweat now pouring down the boy's bronzed face. "Think, my boy," his father said. The light of faith had finally come back into Danso's eyes. "What do people around here do with grasshoppers?"

"What are you talking about?" Motumba's eyes grew to narrowed slits of confusion. "They hate them! People want to get rid of them! They want to kill them! What else would they do?"

"They eat them," Luami said as she stepped up beside Motumba—her little face was the picture of simplicity. "They cook them and roast them and sell them in the marketplace. We see that all the time in town, Motumba."

No one said a word. Instead, they watched Motumba's impatient face change from a mixture of surprise and embarrassment to wonder and excitement, as if he had suddenly stumbled upon the greatest discovery of his life.

Chapter 14

Danso nodded with a touch of shame himself. "She's right, Motumba. People around here eat grasshoppers. In fact, we've eaten them ourselves, so it makes perfect sense." He turned to Abena respectfully. "And we owe it all to your mother. She was the only one who didn't crack under the pressure. She was the only one who didn't panic. If she hadn't come up with this idea, we would be standing here staring at our barren bean field with nothing to show for it."

Grandpa Manu grunted, and then began to chuckle to himself. "I never would have believed it! In all my born days nothing has ever taken me by such surprise. The whole thing was staring us right in the face, and we couldn't see it! You saved the day, Abena!"

Abena smiled sheepishly. "Oh now, stop making such a fuss," she chided her husband and Grandpa Manu. "God is the one who deserves the credit. I just acted on inspiration. I don't know what made me think of such a thing. I guess I just saw all those grasshoppers climbing and crawling over one another, and it reminded me of all the heaps of grasshoppers we see in the roasting pans at the market in town."

Everyone was smiling now with the moment of crisis past, but Motumba just stood looking at the field in silence. "Wow! I really feel bad," he finally said. "I guess I gave up on God. In a matter of minutes I gave up my faith, and stopped believing in all the things we've learned in the past few weeks." He still looked bewildered, but he seemed more disappointed in himself now than anything else.

"It's all right, Motumba. God has blessed us, and that's what really counts," Abena said. She put her arm around Motumba. "And this is going to turn out to be a blessing for people in town too. It's not likely that anyone else will have thought to catch the grasshoppers. They were all too worried about their crops, but now they'll have something to eat."

Danso hung his head too. "Motumba, I know how you feel. This has been hard on all of us, and I have to confess that I've not been a good example for this family today." He scuffed the toe of his sandal in the dirt. "I doubted God. I doubted that He could provide for us, that everything would work out for the best. We wanted God to give us a bean crop so we could sell it. But God gave us 23 bags of grasshoppers to sell at the market instead, and hopefully they'll make up for the bean crop we've lost. The grasshoppers are not beans," he added matter-of-factly, "but people eat them, and God knew there would be less food now that the grasshoppers have destroyed our crops. In the end He has provided a way for us to get some money, and a way for the village to have some food. God always works everything out for the best."

Danso stared up into the bright haze of the morning sunlight. "The earth is the Lord's and everything in it, just like our new book says. Even the grasshoppers," he added, his grimy, dirt-smeared face cracking a smile. "To those of us who trust Him, He will provide. He won't fail us, just as He promised."

He stared at Abena, a look of determination in his eyes. "And you, my wife, have again shown us men what is really important—faith in God's promises." He put his arm around her. "Hard work is necessary, but trusting in God and His goodness is what really matters."

"I never want to doubt God like this again," Motumba said as he stared at the wriggling, bulging sacks of grasshoppers. "The Lord gives and the Lord takes away, but He always surprises us because He always has the last word." He picked up a sack of grasshoppers and raised it to the sky. "When we least expect it, God blesses us in ways we could never guess possible. Blessed be the name of the Lord!"

"Our God shall supply all our needs through His riches in Christ Jesus." Abena smiled as she recited another promise she had been memorizing from the Bible.

With the whole ordeal over, they took their grasshoppers to market. And what a sight they made as they toted the 23 sacks of locusts piled high on a two-wheeled cart. It was quite a load, and it was all they could do to keep the bulging sacks from toppling onto the roadway all the way to town. The whole family followed the old ox as it pulled the cart. Motumba guided Suki while Danso and Grandpa steadied the wobbly load. Abena followed along behind with Abu strapped to her back. Luami skipped ahead, as usual, her eyes and ears open for the little bugs and creatures of God's great big world.

The road to town, which had been recently bordered by green fields and towering trees, now stretched ahead in ruins. It seemed hard to believe that just a few hours ago palm trees and fields of corn had been growing here. Now it was all just a memory. Stripped of every living thing that had once been their covering, the fields lay naked as trees pointed to the sky like bare-boned skeletons. It seemed as if every bird and animal had deserted the area for lack of food or ground cover.

The village folk stared at them as they came into town. What could Danso and his family be doing? Were they moving away? It looked as if their cart were piled high with belongings, and no one could really blame them for leaving. The countryside was all tattered and torn after the grasshopper plague.

But when Danso stopped the cart in the street for a rest, someone noticed that the bags were moving. The children were the first to see it. They stared at the sacks in wonder, and then began pointing excitedly. "There's something moving in those sacks!" they shouted. A crowd immediately began to gather around.

As Motumba had predicted, some looked angry when they saw the sacks of grasshoppers. And why shouldn't they be? The insects served as a reminder of the horrible plague that had just annihilated the countryside. Why on earth would Danso and his family be bringing the horrid things into town?

However, when Danso told them the grasshoppers were food, the worry lines on many faces began to relax, and some even smiled. "There will be little to eat until we can all raise another crop," Danso said encouragingly, "so we'd like to help. We're selling these grasshoppers by the kilo to anyone needing something to eat, and the price will be fair. Just bring your large pots and pans to the market. We'll be roasting them there."

When they reached the marketplace, people stood around watching; some even offered to help unload the grasshoppers. Here was a ready supply of food that would last for weeks when roasted and dried. Why hadn't anyone else thought of this? They could have all collected grasshoppers and made some money, as Danso's family was doing. But it was too late. The grasshoppers were gone, along with their cash crops and food supplies.

Danso set several large caldrons on the ground and filled them with water. Then Motumba built fires under them. When the water was boiling, everybody dumped huge handfuls of the hoppers into the water for a few seconds to kill them. Then they roasted them in shallow pans over open fires. The result was tens of thousands of the crispy grasshoppers ready to eat. The only thing people had to do was pull the wings and legs off the insects before popping them into their mouths.

And of course the Bible did not forbid such a thing. Danso felt good about this latest business venture because grasshoppers were among the food items in the Bible that God mentioned people could eat.

Sure enough, by the end of the week Danso and Abena had sold or bartered away every grasshopper. And they did quite well. In fact, the sale of the grasshoppers brought in more money than they could have earned by selling their beans in the market, twice as much money, they estimated. It was an amazing finish to a totally devastating disaster.

But there were more benefits for the people of Babban Zugu than just grasshoppers to eat. Because of the circumstances, Danso and Abena got to share their newfound faith with sincere village folks who were searching for truth. The story was told again and again about how God brought Kossi to them, and about the book that had changed their lives. The effect was amazing. Even in this time of disaster there were those who were led to see that God's hand is over all His creatures, and that He wants to bless and care for His children.

Kossi soon heard the story through the grapevine. The news about a family in northern Nigeria who had harvested grasshoppers instead of beans was everywhere. He and Pastor Kwame came to see the desolate community and to encourage the families.

"What a disaster!" Pastor Kwame whistled as he stared out across the field on Danso's little farm. "Those little creatures ate everything! Not a green thing is left in the area! What will you do now?"

"We'll plant again soon," Danso smiled, "but for now we'll just pay off all our debts, and put away some of the money for the children's schooling."

"And we'll buy Motumba and Luami shoes," Abena added. "It'll be the first shoes they've had in a long, long time."

Chapter 15

Don't forget to pay your tithe," Pastor Kwame said. "It matters not whether you received an increase from beans or from grasshoppers. Tithe is tithe."

"You're right!" Danso suddenly looked worried. "I can't believe I forgot that! We'll be sure to do that right away! In fact, let me give you the money right now. We don't want God to think we're ungrateful!"

Then he turned to Kossi. "I've been wanting to ask for your help, good friend. Would you be willing to get Motumba started selling books like you do? We want him to earn one of those scholarships you talked about so he can go to a Bible training school."

"I think we can arrange that," Kossi said, grinning at Motumba. "Where would you like him to go to school?"

"Wherever the closest Adventist school is at."

"Well, we have a boarding school in Erunmu. It's a secondary school, which will help Motumba prepare for college classes. You can send him there for two years or maybe less if he does well in the entrance examinations. What about Luami?" Kossi added. He knew the struggle Danso and Abena were having over this issue.

"What do you advise?" Danso asked, not even hesitating.

"I think she should go with Motumba. Luami is so bright. It would be a shame to have her miss an opportunity like this. She can finish preparatory school, and then go right on to high school from there. The two schools are on the same campus. Maybe someday she can even study to be a nurse at the Adventist college." Kossi spoke as if he could see the future and knew of what these two young people could accomplish for God.

"How can we afford all this?" Danso's mind was numb at the thought of all the expenses.

"Motumba can earn all his fees if he works hard during his school breaks. And it's not impossible for a girl to get work in the laundry or as a house helper for one of the teachers at the school. If she can cook, she'll do even better. There's no end of students who want jobs, but good dependable workers are hard to find. Is Luami up to that?"

"I don't know," Danso stated with a faraway look in his eye. "We could ask her."

Luami's eyes shone when Kossi laid out the plan for her schooling. "I could do that!" she said excitedly, and Danso had to smile. Abena had been right. The slow pace of farming would never satisfy Luami. She would soon grow into a woman, and though she would one day marry a young man and have children, that was not her greatest need right now. This was the chance she craved and the challenge that would inspire her to go on to succeed in whatever she felt called to do. This was her opportunity to do great things for God.

That Friday evening they all sat around the campfire and ate roasted grasshoppers while Grandpa told stories he had been reading in the Bible. He told one tale about people in Israel who suffered from grasshopper plagues and lost God's blessing because they weren't faithful in paying their tithe. And he told another story about how God sent a drought on the land because the people worshipped pagan idols. But he also shared stories about people such as Abraham and Jacob, who did as God asked and were blessed for it.

"God has been good to us," Abena said, as Grandpa finished his stories. "We should be very grateful for His blessings on us this week. And now I have a confession to make." She smiled shyly in the dancing firelight. "When the grasshoppers came, I panicked like the rest of you. Not on the outside, but it was there just the same. Like Danso and Motumba, I doubted God. I doubted He could provide for us. I doubted that everything would work out for the best. We wanted God to give us a bean crop so that we could sell it, but He gave us 23 bags of grasshoppers to sell at the market instead.

"God is very wise. He knew there would be no crops or food after the grasshoppers came, so He provided a way for us to get some money and a way for the village folks to have some food. And besides all that, we've been able to be a witness for God in the village because of all this. Already there are those who want to know more about our faith in God and how we have been so strong through all this. Some have even asked me if they can study the Bible with us."

"Praise God!" Danso grinned. "God always works everything out for the best! To those who love Him, He cannot fail, and now our cup runs over. 'Blessed be the name of the Lord!'"

"'Blessed be the name of the Lord!'" the whole family echoed.

"You know," Danso added, "I was just thinking: we often pray for good crops, and we pray that God will send the rain to make our crops grow. But showers of grasshoppers? We would never have thought to pray for such a thing, but that's exactly what we got!"

"Amen!" everyone said, and they all laughed as they finished their treat of roasted grasshoppers around the evening fire.

DON'T FORGET THE SABBATH

Chapter 1

Adamu stood in the shade of the blacksmith's shop waiting for the repairman to fix his handcart. A piece of metal strapping had broken loose from the back of the cart, and the blacksmith was the only man in town who could repair it for him. The cotton crop was fast ripening and would soon be dry enough to harvest, and Adamu needed the handcart to haul his bales of cotton to market.

The day was a scorcher, with no breeze to stir the waves of shimmering heat rising from the dusty pathway outside the shop. Biting flies buzzed everywhere, landing on Adamu's legs and arms and neck. The cotton farmer swatted at the pesky flies impatiently, but they kept coming back to bother him.

"You'll come to work today, or I'll fire you!" A harsh voice cut through the sultry heat of the afternoon air. Adamu leaned his head out the doorway to see Musa, a wealthy villager, with his hands on his hips glaring at Bahija, one of his hired hands.

"But my son Chiamaka is sick, boss!" Bahija kept his head down, fearful of Musa's wrath. "He has dysentery, and I must take him to the doctor at the clinic over in Paza Baba, or he'll get worse!"

"Makes no difference to me!" the hard-hearted man growled. "You agreed to work for me! Ask someone else to take your son to the doctor! Don't you know it's easier for me to hire someone else than to give you the day off!"

Adamu could see the pain in Bahija's eyes. Chiamaka was his oldest son, and it was clear by the look on Bahija's face that the boy needed medical attention. Dysentery wasn't a disease to fool with! Victims of the disease usually got dehydrated until they were too weak to stand! It claimed many lives in the village each year, especially the very young!

But it was obvious that not showing up for work was going to cost Bahija his job. Adamu knew the hired hand had a wife and four small children at home who were dependent on him for food and all of life's needs.

Adamu stepped out into the street and stared at Bahija's boss. Musa was the wealthiest man in Toboni. He owned several large tracts of land, on which he grew mostly cotton. He also had a herd of goats—68 of them, to be exact—and each goat made him infinitely wealthy in the eyes of the villagers. But Musa was also one of the meanest men around. He was a Muslim, but not devout. He obviously cared more for himself than anyone else, least of all the men who worked for him. It seemed he hadn't a sympathetic bone in his body.

"Musa! Why don't you let Bahija take his son to the doctor?" Adamu demanded. "It's clear his son is very sick."

The landowner whirled to glare at Adamu. "Mind your own business!" he growled, eyeing Adamu up and down. "What does this have to do with you! You're a lazy fool yourself! Every Saturday you sit around and do nothing but sing your silly songs and tell crazy stories in that little old broken-down church of yours on the edge of town!"

Adamu was an elder in the local Seventh-day Adventist Church. It was true, every week he and his family did go to the little church and sing songs and tell stories from the Bible. But they didn't do it because they were lazy. They did it because they wanted to honor God's holy Sabbath and were eagerly waiting for the soon coming of Jesus!

Musa turned to Bahija again. "I don't have time to argue with ungrateful employees! If you have to call your friends over here to tell me how to run my business, you can just leave! And this after all I've done for you!" he snorted. "Go on! Get out of here! You're more trouble than you're worth! And take your friend with you!" he added.

"Please, no!" Bahija begged. "It's OK; I'll work!" His shoulders slumped a little lower as he fought to keep his job.

Musa stalked off, and Adamu went to stand by Bahija. "I'm sorry about your son," he said, but the hired hand scowled and turned away.

"Why don't you leave me alone!" he snarled. "You've done enough damage for one day!"

Adamu stared after him, not knowing what to say. This was not turning out as he had thought it would. Instead of helping the poor man out, Adamu had only made things worse! He really felt bad now. It was sad that poor men like Bahija had so few real rights, but that's the way things were in Toboni, a French-speaking African village in northern Togo.

Musa was indeed a hard man. He was an outspoken leader in the community who ridiculed those who disagreed with him. Besides being a bully and treating his workers like dirt, he was especially hateful toward the small group of Adventists in the village. This wasn't the first time he had made fun of Adamu and the other believers in the small congregation. It didn't really make much difference to Adamu whether Musa liked him or not. He didn't have to depend on Musa for his livelihood as many of the other villagers did. Fortunately, Adamu owned a piece of land and worked for himself as a cotton farmer.

But men like Bahija were considered small in Musa's eyes, and not worth much. He was a nobody in Toboni, and the welfare of him and his family mattered little in the landowner's eyes. It seemed so wrong to Adamu, but what could he do? He wasn't anyone important in the village either.

But as Adamu glanced down the street after Bahija's departing figure, he suddenly had a thought. "Wait! Bahija!" he called. "I've got an idea!" He felt badly for the hired hand and his family. He hadn't meant to meddle, but he hated to see people mistreated, especially by Musa, the richest, meanest man in town.

Adamu hurried to catch up with Bahija. The poor man scowled at Adamu again until he heard him blurt out, "Why don't you let me take Chiamaka to the doctor in Paza Baba. I'll see that he gets there and back safely. Dysentery is a serious illness!" Adamu added sympathetically. "If you don't get your son to the doctor right away, he could even die." He laid a hand on Bahija's shoulder. "And besides, I have to do some business in Paza Baba anyway."

Bahija was stunned at Adamu's offer and couldn't answer at first, but then he finally found his voice. "You would do this for me?" he stammered.

"Absolutely! Anything for a brother in need! You deserve better treatment than you're getting." Adamu smiled at the troubled father.

Bahija looked surprised, but Adamu waved him off. "Go to work. I'll get your son and take him to Paza Baba."

Helping Bahija was the finest thing Adamu could have done, and to Bahija it meant the world. It was not every day that someone could save his job and rescue his child from danger at the same time. A new friendship was formed that day, one that served as a springboard for fulfilling the poor man's deeper needs. Before many days had passed Adamu was talking to Bahija about the goodness of God, and the need to forgive his enemies, and how to have lasting peace in his heart. This led to Bible studies, and then Adamu invited Bahija to church with him.

This posed problems for Bahija, of course. Musa grew angry when he heard Bahija's request for the day off. Musa insisted that Bahija could not miss work, especially not to worship in the little church at the edge of town. "If you insist on taking Saturday off, you're fired!" he told Bahija gruffly.

The village shaman didn't help any, either. "What are you doing following that crazy new religion!" the old witch doctor said as he scowled at Bahija in the market. "It's the strangest thing in all of Togo! Worshipping the Lord God on the seventh day of the week instead of the first! The good spirits will be angry for sure, and so will the priests who come on their circuit through Tchamba, Guidan Agoulou, and Paza Baba!"

But Adamu told Bahija not to worry. "If you're faithful to God," he said with a light in his eyes, "the Lord will bless you far beyond anything you're receiving at your present job. I should know," he exclaimed. "When I gave my heart to God, it changed my life just as it's changing yours."

And it all turned out just as Adamu said it would. Bahija went to church with Adamu, and the next day a man knocked on Bahija's door to ask him if he could begin work immediately on another farm not far from where Adamu lived. "The boss, Monsieur Eli, will pay you 3600 CFA a week."

"Thirty-six hundred CFA!" Bahija whistled to himself. That was more than what he was making working for Musa.

"I'll take it!" Bahija said excitedly. "When does he need me?"

"As soon as you can begin."

"Tell Monsieur Eli I'll be there within the hour!" And with that Bahija dashed off to Adamu's farm to tell him the good news.

"God always blesses us when we do as He asks and honor Him first in our lives," Adamu said with a smile. "Now go, Bahija, and make Monsieur Eli very glad he hired you to work for him."

Chapter 2

Helping his neighbors was nothing new for Adamu. He had been doing this for years. In fact, it was the way the Seventh-day Adventist Church had gotten started in Toboni, through the hard work and spiritual dedication of Adamu himself.

But Adamu hadn't always been an Adventist. A dozen years before, he had become interested in Christianity when he ended up in an Adventist hospital in Lomé. He had been to the city to see an uncle when he had an attack of appendicitis and needed immediate surgery. The Seventh-day Adventists treated him well, and their kindness drew him to their faith. When he was released from the hospital, they promised to send a man to Toboni to teach Adamu more about their beliefs.

Three months later, to Adamu's surprise, a man named Edem Olivier arrived in town looking for him. Adamu was so excited and asked Edem to sit down then and there, to teach him everything he knew about the Bible.

"That's a great idea!" Edem laughed. "But I've got a better idea! Let's find a place where I can preach to a large crowd."

The two of them set to work immediately. There was no Adventist church in Toboni for them to meet in, so they just chose a spot under a big tree. Then they built a platform of bricks and invited everyone in town to come.

The meetings were a success from the first night. Edem had a powerful voice that could be heard far and wide without a microphone, and when he preached people showed up out of curiosity, if for nothing else.

And Adamu was there each night to support him. After his long days in the hot sun hoeing and weeding his fields, the cool night air felt good on his face as he sat by lantern light and listened to Edem. The first few nights Edem spoke about strange beasts from Daniel and Revelation. But there were other interesting topics too from the rest of the Bible, such as how God made the world and why Jesus came to die for the sins of the world.

When Edem told the people he had books that covered the topics he preached about, Adamu was especially interested and was the first in line to buy them. He bought two books—a Bible and *La Tragédie des Siècle,* a

French translation of the book *The Great Controversy*. The book told all about the history and struggles of God's church—Adamu could hardly put it down. His craving for truth knew no bounds, and he found he could not get enough of spiritual truth. It was as if these books were water to his thirsty soul.

At night after the meetings were over, Adamu and Edem would talk, often into the wee hours of the morning. Adamu had no family in Toboni, so he invited Edem to stay with him during the series of meetings. Adamu's mother and father had died when he was young, leaving him the small farm he now lived on. He wasn't married yet, and his sister and extended family lived in the big city, so Adamu could spend all his spare time studying with Edem.

There were others in town who bought books too—eight families in all, and when they heard that Edem was studying with Adamu, they wanted him to have Bible studies with them too. Edem suggested they all study together at Adamu's house in the early evening before the meeting began. Adamu especially liked that. It was as though he had a family again.

Soon they were studying twice a week on Wednesdays and Saturdays. Edem knew his Bible well and seemed to make it come alive when they studied. Everything made sense when he explained it in the simple language of the village folks. And he knew so many stories! The children in the group especially enjoyed that part of the meetings. Edem's stories about Noah's flood and Moses parting the Red Sea and the walls of Jericho falling down seemed so real when he told them.

The group also discussed the things they were reading in the books Edem had sold them. Besides *The Great Controversy*, they had a book titled *Jesus Christ*, a French version of *The Desire of Ages*. Everyone loved that book because it was all about the life of Jesus.

Sometimes Edem read to the group and sometimes Adamu did. The group enjoyed hearing Adamu read because he had a deep resonant voice. "You are a born leader," Edem told him one night after the meeting. "God has given you a gift—you hold the attention of these people so easily. I'm praying God will inspire you to do great things for Him in this village."

At the regular evening meetings Edem spoke on some really interesting topics. One night he preached about worshipping God on Saturdays instead of Sundays, and things began to click in Adamu's mind. When he had been in the hospital in Lomé, he had heard the nurses talking about the Sabbath, and he had wondered what it was all about. He had also heard of people in the neighboring country of Ghana who had the strange custom of worshipping God on Saturdays. For centuries it was said the Ghanaians worshipped like this every seventh day without fail, rain or shine. Other Christian groups in West Africa worshipped on the first day of the week, but not the Ghanaian Sabbathkeepers.

And now here was this follower of God giving proof after proof that the seventh day of the week was indeed God's holy Sabbath. And the most intriguing thing about the Sabbath was that these ideas were all in the Bible. As plain as the great yellow moon rising up over the eastern horizon each night.

Adamu received the Sabbath truth, and everything else just fell into place: the knowledge about what happens to people when they die, the idea of returning to God a faithful tithe of all that is earned, the amazing discovery that Jesus is now in the heavenly sanctuary preparing for His soon return to earth.

Gratefully Adamu accepted Jesus as his Savior, and then he began doing what anyone would do with such good news. He began sharing what he had learned with his neighbors and friends. Of course, many of them had been to the meetings, and had been interested in the many topics Edem preached about. But not everyone was like Adamu. Not everyone could see with such clear conviction the great Bible truths, and they were slower to listen and learn. Adamu felt a burden for these folks and often talked to them about their salvation. Some were annoyed at the persistence of his arguments, while others laughed. But the families he and Edem had studied with were sincere and were searching for truth like Adamu was.

Adamu and several others knew they should be baptized, but Edem could not baptize them because he was not a preacher. When he finally left he promised to send someone who could perform the baptism ceremony. Adamu continued studying with the interested families and even conducted worship services for them.

Finally, several months later an Adventist preacher came to town to baptize Adamu and his fellow brothers and sisters in Christ. It was a high day Adamu knew he would never forget as long as he lived. Eight people were baptized and began their new life with Jesus. The joy on their faces was complete.

There was no church building for them to meet in each Sabbath, so they continued meeting at Adamu's house. Little by little the numbers grew. From this nucleus the group became a company, and the company became a fledgling church.

As membership increased, it became evident that the group needed a building to meet in, so Adamu organized the members to help build a little church. Concrete was expensive for poor farmers, but the Lord blessed them, and they somehow scraped the money together to buy the bags of cement. Evenings and weekends Adamu led a crew in making the cement blocks they needed for the walls, and block by block the building went up. The little congregation thought they would build a thatched, palm-frond roof, but Adamu said they must do it right. And so they scrimped and saved some more and bargained for the sheets of tin they needed to cover the roof. It wasn't a large church when it was finished, but it was their church.

Adamu sent word to Edem and asked him to come hold more evangelistic meetings in the little church, but Edem could not come. Finally after months of waiting and hoping, Adamu decided to conduct the meetings himself. He didn't consider himself at all qualified, but he wanted the church to grow, so he just prayed that God would bless him in his efforts.

And he surprised himself at how much success he had. It was in his first campaign, that his best friend, Hassan, another cotton farmer, was baptized. The second campaign brought in two young women who were sisters, and it was these girls who later became Adamu's and Hassan's wives. Lantana and Talatu had the qualities every good African man was looking for. They came from hardworking families and knew how to make all the great African foods: foufou, kenkey, and kokonte. Talatu was the older of the two, but it was Lantana's bright smile that stole Adamu's heart.

Chapter 3

A nd that's how Adamu came to be such an evangelist in the little town of Toboni. The little church they had built was thriving now with 72 members. A few of the members had shops in the village of Toboni, and some were merchants who bought and sold dry goods. But most of the members were poor farmers, and most had no more than a hectare or two of land to farm.

All told, most of the folks in the church could trace their conversion stories to Adamu and his persistent missionary work, and Bahija was just one of them. The new concept of Sabbath came easy for Bahija, probably because he had received good fortune so soon after taking his stand for God. But there were other areas that were not so easily conquered in Bahija's life. Fear of the spirits, and the worship of the dead, were perfect examples.

"I'm going to Sokode this weekend," Bahija told Adamu one evening during their Bible study. "Unfortunately, I'll have to miss going to church with you and your family."

"Well, it's a shame you'll have to miss church here. Maybe you can find an Adventist church in Sokode," Adamu said with concern.

"Oh, I won't have time for church," Bahija quickly added. "We're going to be pretty busy with holiday celebrations."

"Doing what?"

"The usual stuff. Eating. Feasting and drinking with my family. Most of them live in Sokode. I'll try to keep from drinking too much, but we have to drink to the health of our ancestors, you know." Bahija rubbed his stomach, and his face grew bright in anticipation.

Adamu didn't say what he was thinking about the drinking. He was worried that Bahija would miss church, but he was worried about something much more serious. "I think there's a problem here," he finally said, looking straight at Bahija. "I don't think you should go to that feast this weekend. In fact, from now on I think you'd be wise to give up such holidays altogether."

"Why should I do that?" Bahija asked in surprise.

"Because feast day celebrations that honor spirit and ancestor worship are no safe place for a Christian to be at."

"Well, I have to go!" Bahija set his jaw stubbornly. "I have to go! It's a family tradition! If I don't go, my father will be very angry! My family has been keeping this holiday for generations! It's the backbone of my tribe!" Adamu was surprised at Bahija's tone of voice, as if he didn't care what Adamu said or thought. It was strange that Bahija could forget so quickly all the kindnesses Adamu had shown him.

But Adamu wouldn't give up. "It doesn't matter," he countered, hoping Bahija would change his mind. "God is asking you not to go. He has forbidden His people from honoring the spirits of devils and dead people, and that's what you'll be doing. The Bible is very clear about all this."

Adamu began leafing through the pages of the Bible. "It says so right here," he added as he found a famous passage that detailed the very thing they were talking about. "'And when they say to you, "Seek those who are mediums and wizards, who whisper and mutter," should not a people seek their God? Should they seek the dead on behalf of the living?' You can read it for yourself in Isaiah 8:19," Adamu said.

"The Bible says that?" Bahija's eyes grew wide.

"It does, and with good reason." Adamu stared intently at Bahija. "Spirit worship has always been a problem in this old world. It was a problem for the Israelites in the land of Canaan during Bible times too. It's all in the Bible. I guess God knew you and I would need to know about the forces of darkness today in this century just as people needed to know about the evil practice back in ancient times. That's why He recorded all those stories for us."

Bahija didn't say anything.

"God's orders about what to do to get rid of the sorcery and witchcraft in those days was pretty serious business," Adamu said as he turned the pages of his Bible again. "God says here in Deuteronomy 18:10 that His people were not supposed to allow anyone who practiced such things to live in the land. 'There shall not be found among you anyone who makes his son or his daughter pass through the fire,' Adamu read, 'or one who practices witchcraft, or a soothsayer, or one who interprets omens, or a sorcerer.'"

Bahija couldn't read, but he leaned over to look at the words Adamu was pointing at.

"Later it became the law in Israel that any sorcerer or witch who continued to practice their trade should be executed," Adamu added. "That's what it was like in those days."

"Kill all the spirit worshippers! We can't do that!" Bahija protested. "And we can't make them move out of the country! This is my family we're talking about!"

"No we can't, and we shouldn't," Adamu said, almost smiling. "That's not our job today, but we can refuse to take part in any of these ancient rites that are as evil as Satan himself."

Bahija hung his head. "I'll be honest with you," he admitted. "I'm afraid of the spirits and the dead. I'm afraid of their power and what they can do."

Adamu nodded in the light of the kerosene lamp. "It's true, the spirits do have a lot of power, but if you worship the God of heaven, you don't need to worry about them. Now the dead? That's another story altogether," the church leader sighed. "We don't have time to get into a long discussion about that tonight, but let me assure you, Bahija, that the dead can't hurt you. In fact, according to the Bible they know nothing at all because they are sleeping. It's the evil spirits and demons that make all the trouble for us."

"Do you have any verses that talk about that?" Bahija asked almost timidly. He glanced over his shoulder into the shadows of the night as though he were afraid the evil spirits might hear him.

"Yes, I do!" Adamu laid a hand on Bahija's shoulder. "I'll read you one of my favorites. Paul talks about the spirit world in the book of Romans." Adamu turned the pages of his Bible again. "He says there is evil all around us and that the evil spirits would take our eternal salvation from us if they could, but they can't. Listen to this. 'For I am persuaded that neither death nor life, nor angels nor principalities nor powers, nor things present nor things to come, nor height nor depth, nor any other created thing, shall be able to separate us from the love of God which is in Christ Jesus our Lord'" (Rom. 8:38).

Bahija began to relax. "I feel safe when you read from the Bible," he told Adamu.

"You are safe," Adamu replied, "but not because of anything I do. It's because the Spirit of God is here tonight in this room, bringing you the peace of heaven. And nothing can harm you when the power of Jesus is in a place."

"This is all so new to me." Bahija shook his head. "I don't know what to say!"

"Just believe," Adamu urged him. "Sometimes it's best just to take God at His word and believe."

Bahija put his head in his hands. "So what am I going to do? All my family gives offerings and pours out the holy water to the ancestors during the festive holidays. And they expect me to do it too." He really looked worried now.

"Well, the first thing you need to decide is if you are going to obey God. Just like with the Sabbath, you need to do as God's commandments tell us, even if it costs a lot. There are many stories in the Bible that encourage us to do that. Like the tale of three young men who were true to God and refused to bow down to a king's giant image of gold, even though they got thrown into a burning brick kiln for it."

"A brick kiln! Wow! That's pretty hot! I guess that ended their foolishness. I bet anyone who saw the execution that day learned a lesson about disobeying the king."

Adamu smiled. "You're right. Everyone did learn a lesson, but not one you may think. You see, they didn't burn up."

"Didn't burn up?" Bahija looked confused. "Why not? Was the fire out in the furnace?"

"Oh no; it was fired up and hot as could be." Adamu squinted in the lamplight. "In fact, it was hot enough to kill all the soldiers who threw the young men in. They died instantly from the heat!"

Bahija stared at Adamu in disbelief. "I don't get it. Did they have some kind of magic power to withstand the heat? Did they carry an amulet or good-luck charm for protection?"

Adamu tapped his Bible. "Their protection came from the Word of God."

Bahija's eyes grew wide again. "The Bible?"

"That's right, my friend. When we believe God's Word and trust that He will keep His promises, which are all in this good book, we have all the power in the world we need. Listen to what one of God's apostles said about those who serve God as His witnesses in the last days of earth's history. 'They will take up serpents; and if they drink anything deadly, it will by no means hurt them; they will lay hands on the sick, and they will recover.' That's found in Mark 16:18."

"Amazing!" Bahija could hardly believe what he was hearing. "Seems the Bible has everything we need."

"Seems it does," Adamu repeated, and the Holy Spirit echoed his words.

The two men could feel God's presence very near that night as the crickets chirped and the soft evening wind blew in through the open window.

All these new ideas brought wonderful life changes for Bahija. He learned new truths from the Bible every week, and each day his faith and trust in Jesus grew. It was hard to give up the old ways sometimes, but every time he accepted some new gem of the gospel story he was always surprised at the blessings God brought into his life.

"Sooner than you think, you'll be telling others the good news of salvation," Adamu told Bahija. "It will just well up inside of you and have to get out. And when that happens God will use you as a missionary to bring others to Him just as I brought you to Jesus."

And Adamu was right, although Bahija had no idea just how soon his prediction would come true.

Chapter 4

I have a friend who needs help," Bahija told Adamu one day after church. "His daughter died while we were in Sokode, and he is beside himself with grief. Will you come with me and see him today?"

"Absolutely." Adamu's face grew troubled. "How did she die?"

"She was hit by a car. My friend and his family live on a quiet city street of Sokode. They live in a wooden shack he built for his family on a vacant lot that he pays a small amount of money for each month. Many important people live on that street—embassy people, police officials, missionaries, and rich businesspeople. It's one of those streets with a compound wall around each home.

"Anyway, one of the government officials who lives on that street drives a black government car with a yellow license plate. The plate allows him to come and go as he pleases without the police stopping him all the time, as they do ordinary people."

"What's your friend's name?" Adamu smiled at Bahija's tendency to wander with all the details of his story.

"Oh, sorry," Bahija smiled. "His name is Emmanuel. Anyway, the government official's son also drives the car sometimes. He's only 17 or 18, I think, and he usually drives too fast. All the children play on that street, so it's very dangerous! I've told Emmanuel many times to move off that street, but he told me he doesn't have any better place to go. He always says he will go one day when he can get the money."

Adamu's face grew serious. "And the boy hit Emmanuel's daughter?" It was obvious where this story was going.

Bahija nodded slowly. "I was there and saw the whole thing happen. The kids came running in, screaming that Tinde had been hit. Emmanuel's wife let out a wail that could've woken the dead! Everyone was running around in a panic! The young man got out of his car and was pretty upset himself, not knowing what to do as he stared at the little girl on the street with blood coming out of her mouth. He just watched as Emmanuel and his wife, Bijou, both fell down in the street beside the little girl, groaning and moaning and clutching at her pitifully.

"They were there for I don't know how long, and then something snapped in Emmanuel, and he went crazy! I think it finally hit him what had actually happened! He suddenly grabbed a machete from a gardener standing nearby and went after the young man to kill him! And he would have if we hadn't dragged him away! Emmanuel was screaming and cursing, but we finally wrestled him to the ground and managed to get the machete out of his hand."

Bahija's eyes were wide. It was obvious Bahija was reliving the moments of that day as if he were still there.

"But Emmanuel is a strong man!" Bahija continued. "He broke loose from our grip and ran down the street. We didn't know what he was going to do, so we quickly took the young man inside the gate of one of the homes. Sure enough, a minute later Emmanuel came running back up the street with another machete. He could see the young man inside the gate, so he tried to climb over it. We had to wrestle him to the ground again to get that machete away too.

"All the while Emmanuel was screaming and moaning, looking to heaven and crying out, 'Why, God! Why!' It was the saddest thing I think I've ever seen." Bahija finally ended his story and grew quiet.

"What was the little girl's name again?" Adamu asked, shaking his head sadly.

"Tinde. She was a sweet little thing. Only 6. She had so much life in her, and Emmanuel is so distraught now. I'm afraid he is going to do something desperate!"

"Then we must go and see him."

"I can arrange that—we'll have to go by car. It's the least I can do for my friend."

The two men didn't even eat dinner after church. They took some pâtés and papayas in a sack, and immediately caught a ride to the city.

"We may have to stay the night," Bahija said as they traveled. "It all depends on how it goes with Emmanuel."

"God will take care of the details," Adamu replied. "We are on a mission for Him, and that's all that matters. Jesus would have done the same for us."

They arrived in Sokode before dark and caught a taxi to the quiet street where Emmanuel lived at the edge of town. The sun was just setting when they arrived, and Adamu could hear the sounds of evening rising on the breeze. Cicadas scraped out their tunes in the trees along the road, and down in the valley where a stand of banana trees grew, he could hear a pair of cuckoos calling to each other mournfully.

Upon arrival at Emmanuel's home they found him sitting outside by the little cast-iron burner his family used for cooking their meager meals. When Emmanuel saw Bahija, he jumped up quickly. "What are you doing here?" he asked in surprise.

"We came to see you," Bahija said quietly. "We know you have suffered much, and I asked my friend Adamu if he would come to the city with me to see if there is anything we can do to help." The two men shook hands, and Emmanuel nodded graciously.

"Adamu is a very spiritual man," Bahija added, "and he is a leader in our church back home."

"Thank you for coming," Emmanuel said quietly. "Please have a seat." He glanced around at his humble home in embarrassment. "Our house is simple, but what we have is yours."

"How is Bijou?" Bahija asked respectfully.

"Not so good." Emmanuel gestured in the direction of their one-room shack. "She is sleeping now and seems to be doing a lot of that lately."

"My wife was like too that when she lost a child at birth," Bahija said. "She was overcome with sadness for days. I had a hard time getting her to do anything. She wouldn't eat or come out and spend time with the family. She couldn't even work. She just lay on her sleeping mat all day long."

Emmanuel frowned. "That's pretty much the way it is with Bijou. She does come out and get the meals ready for the children, and she gives them baths every night like she always has, but then she goes back in and lies down again."

Bahija laid a hand on Emmanuel's shoulder comfortingly. "Adamu and I have come to pray with you and encourage you. Will that be OK?"

"Thank you." Emmanuel hung his head. "You are kind."

Bahija looked to Adamu to lead out, but Adamu simply nodded at Bahija. "You go ahead for now," he said. "You're doing fine."

They all bowed their heads, and Bahija prayed a simple prayer from his heart. "Lord, we are so sad for Emmanuel and Bijou. They have lost their little girl, whom You loved so much. It's not fun living in this world where there is so much sadness. Please be with Emmanuel and his family that they will know how to deal with all the pain. You lived here like us many years ago, Lord, so You know how it is. Comfort Bijou in her time of sorrow, and give her strength so she can go on living and caring for her children."

By the time Bahija had finished, darkness had fallen, as it does so quickly near the equator. The fire flickered weakly in the little cast-iron burner, and Emmanuel added some more charcoal. It was such a peaceful night out. If it hadn't been for the circumstances of the occasion, they would have really enjoyed the evening.

"Emmanuel, what do you do for work?" Adamu asked, finally breaking the silence.

"I'm in construction," Emmanuel responded as he stared into the fire. "I work on projects in small towns surrounding Sokode, so I'm gone all week. I'm home only on the weekends."

"Construction is a good field," Adamu said. "It offers a man a chance to do a day's work for an honest wage."

"Yes, and we need the money," Emmanuel added. "Especially with the cost of the funeral." He paused as if wanting to say more, but hesitated since Adamu was a stranger.

"Being away from your wife must be hard right now," Adamu stated matter-of-factly. "We have to be the strong ones and go on providing for the family, but they don't always understand that, especially during hard times. All they see is their own pain and how bad things have gotten."

Emmanuel glanced up at Adamu. *Who is this man Bahija has brought with him?* he wondered. This stranger seemed amazingly perceptive, and he found himself wanting to open up more. Such a thing wasn't typical for Emmanuel, or any African man, for that matter, but Emmanuel couldn't believe how good it felt to get all his worries off his chest.

Chapter 5

You're quite right!" Emmanuel sighed. He dished up some of the rice and peanut sauce left over from supper that night and offered it to his visitors. "It's not been easy. My little girl's death has been hard for all of us. Bijou doesn't want me to leave her alone anymore, but my boss said I need to work if I want to keep my job."

Adamu nodded. "And I suppose he has 10 others waiting to fill your shoes if you decide to stay home with your wife?"

"Exactly." Emmanuel glanced at Adamu again, but Adamu only stared into the fire. "I have two boys, both older than Tinde," Emmanuel continued. "They are trying to do their part and help their mother in her grief, but she needs me at home too. This feeling of loss just will not let her go! She cannot shake it! Just this weekend my wife asked that I not go away anymore to work with the construction crew."

Emmanuel took a deep breath and continued on, sharing the severity of his wife's grief. "While I was away last week, Bijou said the spirit of our daughter, Tinde, came to visit her every night. Tinde tells Bijou she is lonely and cold and wants my wife to go with her. She stands in the doorway of our home and holds out her hand, beckoning Bijou to follow her. Of course, my wife is terrified because she knows this can only mean one thing. If she gives in and goes with Tinde, then she will walk from this life into the next and never come back."

Emmanuel continued staring into the fire. "The first few nights she said she panicked at Tinde's invitation. She knows she has to help care for the boys and me. She loves us all and that has helped a little to keep her going. But she confessed that with every passing night she is growing weaker in her determination to stay. Each time Tinde comes Bijou grows more used to the idea of leaving this world. Night before last she was so depressed she thought she would just give up the fight and go, but the thought of me coming back home the next day kept her strong for one more day."

Emmanuel paused, and the stillness of the night pressed in around them. The charcoal in the burner was now only a few glowing embers, and the night birds had all gone to sleep. Even the crickets were quiet.

"Are you a Christian?" Adamu asked.

"I'm a Catholic, but my wife isn't. She believes in the worship of spirits and the veneration of our ancestors who have passed on before us."

"Do you believe in spirits?"

Emmanuel paused, not sure how to answer the question. "I fear them," he finally said.

"Did you know that there are good spirits as well as evil spirits?" Adamu added. "The good spirits are sent by God to help protect us. They are called angels. The evil spirits are also angels, but fallen ones who rebelled against God long ago."

"I didn't know that." Emmanuel glanced around him into the darkness as if aware that the spirits might be listening in on their conversation.

"If we trust in God, He will protect us from the evil spirits, because God's holy angels are many, many times more powerful than the evil angels."

Emmanuel didn't reply.

"God asks that we trust in Him. He loves you, Emmanuel, and He doesn't want you to fear death or the evil spirits. Can you put your faith in God and believe that?"

"I don't know. I try, but it's hard. I guess I'm not a very good Catholic. The Catholic Church here in Togo doesn't care what you worship or how. They just want us to take part in the sacraments of Mass and the holy water rituals."

"That is a problem, Emmanuel. Your church doesn't teach you the things I am telling you about because most of the priests don't believe in everything the Bible teaches." Adamu laid a hand on Emmanuel's shoulder. "Do you believe in prayer?"

"Yes, I think prayer has power, but the priest always tells us we need to come to him to pray. I have not been taught to pray."

"Do you believe that Jesus is the Son of God?"

"Of course."

"Did you know that Jesus told us how to pray to the Father in heaven?"

Emmanuel was quiet for a moment. "I did not know that."

"Would you like us to pray with you again and teach you how to pray?"

"You would do that?"

"Absolutely. Prayer can give you real power. It can help deliver you from sickness and evil spirits and even death."

They all bowed their heads, and Adamu lifted his heart to God for help like he had never done before. "Our Father who is in heaven, thank You for Your Son, Jesus. Thank You that He came to this world to deliver us from the evil one's power. We put our trust in You, Father, because You have all power in heaven and earth. We pray now for Emmanuel and Bijou, and we pray for their two boys. Please help them in this great time of loneliness, and protect them from the evil one. We ask all these things in the name of Jesus. Amen."

Adamu lifted his head. "And now we must go, Emmanuel. It is late, and we have yet to go to Bahija's brother's home, where we will spend the night. But we will stay in touch," he added quickly. "I'll be asking Bahija from time to time how you and Bijou are doing. We hope we have helped encourage you on the road to heaven."

The men shook hands again, and then Adamu and Bahija disappeared into the shadows of the night.

"I'm worried about Emmanuel," Bahija confessed the next morning on the ride back to Toboni. "He is so weak, and he knows so little about the great truths of the Bible. I'm not even sure He believes half the things we told him last night."

"He will grow," Adamu stated. "You are a true missionary, Bahija, and Emmanuel has been blessed because of your concern for his well-being."

"But he is still so far from the truth!" protested Bahija. "His wife still believes in the power of the spirits. They are both very superstitious and will do anything the priest tells them to do. He doesn't know a thing about the Sabbath, or what really happens to people when they die. And how can he be ready for the coming of Jesus if he doesn't even know about it?"

Adamu smiled at Bahija. "All in God's good time, my friend. We must give Emmanuel time to think of the things we've said. You've planted the seed with God's help, and someday Emmanuel will be ready to hear more. But not now. He is still so stunned over the loss of his daughter. Give him time, Bahija. Be patient like God."

Bahija bowed his head humbly. "I pray that God will help me do that."

Chapter 6

By now Adamu and Lantana had four children—two boys and two girls—Sena, Lucien, Bella, and Kafui. Hassan and Talatu had three children, all of them boys. Children are a blessing for African families because there are many everyday chores to be done. Girls usually help with the cooking and laundry and younger children, and boys help with the farmwork.

Adamu and Hassan had their own land and were hard workers, so they were better off than most families. Adamu had five hectares and Hassan had four, and this kept them busy. According to world standards, these plots of land were small, but cotton farming was not easy, and they had to put in many hours of labor to help turn out a crop.

Adamu knew his boys were a godsend, and the family farm thrived with their help. Sometimes he would take Sena and Lucien to help Hassan with the work on his farm, and sometimes Hassan and his sons returned the favor. Some months of the year it seemed that there was not enough time to finish all the work in the fields, such as during the harvest, and then the girls had to come out and help too. Fortunately, school was not held during the busiest times of the year.

Some families had no sons, so the girls had to work in the fields all the time, and although necessary, that could be hard. Sadly, some farmers in Africa exploited their children and seemed to think work was all children were good for. Adamu and Hassan tried to raise their children differently. "Work can be a blessing, even if it just keeps us out of trouble," Adamu always told his children. "Watch the ants. They work harder than all of us. If you work hard like them, God will bless you. You don't want your life to be a playground for the devil."

But to the people of Togo, the importance of children went beyond the everyday lessons of life. Children represented a passing of the torch to the next generation, and for their little Adventist church, Adamu and Hassan knew this was very important. If raised well, children could go on to serve God in bigger ways outside the family circle. Adamu wanted his own children to go to a Christian boarding school, and then on to the Adventist seminary in Lomé so they could learn how to sell Christian books and give Bible studies like Edem did. If they could sell books for a scholarship, they might even get to go to college to become a pastor or teacher or nurse.

To help prepare them for such dreams, Adamu and Hassan made sure there were lots of activities in the church so the young people would have opportunities to practice their faith. They organized the youth group to help older folks in town with their small gardens. They helped the kids raise money to purchase Christmas gifts for the children at the local orphanage run by the Catholic nuns. They even taught their children to give Bible studies to interested families.

One of the greatest blessings for Adamu and his friends when they became Adventists was the good news of the Sabbath. Every seventh day they rested from all their labors. The Sabbath was a wonderful way to escape the drudgery of hard work, especially for the farmers of the congregation. Nearly everyone grew cotton, and that kind of farming required strenuous, backbreaking, dawn-to-dusk labor in the outdoors. It meant preparing the fields early in the season and planting the cotton in long rows that stretched to the edges of the field. It meant hoeing the stubborn weeds that pushed their way up through the red-brown soil. It meant snatching pesky weevils off the plants that would destroy the cotton. And so, after a long week of work planting or hoeing or picking bugs off the plants, the Sabbath was always a great relief!

"The Sabbath is the best medicine for our tired, worn-out bodies, but it's more than that," Adamu would always say. "It's a commandment of God, and we're forbidden to do any work on that day! God knew exactly what He was doing when He told us, 'Thou shalt not do any work, thou, nor thy son, nor thy daughter' [Ex. 20:10, KJV], and I'm sure He meant you too, Lantana," Adamu would finish, smiling at his wife. "You work harder than all of us put together."

But the best part of the Sabbath was the chance they all had to come together and worship God in their small church on the edge of town. Friends and family within the church saw one another often during the week, but on Sabbath they could sing praises to God and pray and encourage one another as they looked forward to the soon coming of Jesus.

Cotton farming was a poor man's game. Money was always tight. Although most farmers raised two crops of cotton a year, there was rarely any money for extras. If it was a good year, they usually got by, but if a drought set in, the crops suffered. Then everybody had to help forage in the forests and fields for wild roots and berries and the odd antelope they could hunt down with a bow and arrow.

Fortunately, this was a good year—the cotton farmers of Toboni couldn't have asked for better conditions. As harvesttime rolled around, the weather was perfect, and everyone prepared to reap what they had sown. Early one morning when the sun's golden disk was well up over the horizon and the fields were dry enough, the farmers all began the big task of picking cotton. It seemed as if the whole village turned out to help the farmers—men and women, kids and older folks. It was wonderful when everyone worked together like this.

They walked the long rows dragging their large sacks behind them and snatching the cotton from the plants, one tuft at a time. The very young children weren't allowed to help pick the cotton. If the prickling thorns snagged their little fingers and hands, they would get blood on the pure white balls of cotton, and then it would be ruined.

When a sack was full, it was taken to the sheds to be picked clean of the little sticks, leaves, and seeds that clung to the cotton balls. That in itself was a tedious job, and it usually took as long to clean the cotton as it did to pick it. But the shade of the cool sheds was always a welcome break from the hot sun, and even the little ones could help with this task.

When the cotton was finally cleared of all the debris, it was tied in big heavy bales. The bales were so big they had to be moved with handcarts and then stacked in the shed where they would stay dry until the government truck could pick them up.

The job of picking cotton was a strenuous one, but it was a fun time, too. By the end of the week village family members were coming from far and wide to help. Adamu's sister showed up, and so did some of his cousins and his uncle Yao from the city.

They laughed and talked as they worked; some even sang lively African folk songs. And in the evenings after dark, tired as they were from dragging the heavy sacks down the long rows of cotton, they always enjoyed the good food prepared by the grandmas of the village. And before bedtime there was always time for a story or two told by one of the old village elders. Of course, by the time the story was finished, the little children were fast asleep on their parents' laps or curled up on a blanket on the ground.

The next morning they were all up again at dawn, ready to get into the fields for another day of work. It was hard labor, especially when the great round sun climbed high in the sky to scorch the cotton pickers, but by the third and fourth days of picking, everyone had their second wind. The goal now was to get finished. With the end in sight, it seemed that nothing could stop them. The sooner the cotton was picked, the sooner they could be done with the fieldwork in the hot sun.

Unless of course, that something was the arrival of the Sabbath. Adamu was firm about that, and so was Hassan. "I hope we can finish by Friday, but if we can't, we'll all be in church on Sabbath, not out here in the fields."

Sure enough, when Friday arrived and they still hadn't finished picking the cotton, the two men told all the family helpers that Saturday would be a day off for them to rest. Others in the village might go on picking their crop during the Sabbath hours, but not them.

"You're a fool!" Uncle Yao fumed when Adamu told everyone to go home early on Friday evening to prepare for the Sabbath. "We should be able to finish in another day or so. The weather tomorrow looks to be good enough, but what if it rains on Sunday? The damp weather will set you back at least a day! Maybe two!"

"I don't care!" Adamu said firmly. "If it should rain and the crop gets damaged, or even ruined completely, I'll not dishonor God's Sabbath. He made the day holy, and I aim to keep it that way just as He commanded."

"Then we'll pick the cotton for you!" Uncle Yao insisted. "We're not seven-day keepers, or whatever it is you call yourself!"

But Adamu wouldn't hear of it, and no amount of arguing could convince him to change his mind.

Chapter 7

Saturday morning came, and Adamu and Hassan went to church with their families just as they said they would. Bathed and dressed in their very best, they were intent on receiving the Lord's blessing. Along the way they met their neighbors who were heading for the fields.

"You can't be serious!" the neighbors said, their faces showing surprise that Adamu and Hassan were really going to go through with their day of rest.

"One day off won't hurt the cotton," Adamu said confidently. "We've got business to tend to in the Lord's house."

"If you lose a day, you might not get the crop in on time!" an old farmer warned them.

"God will take care of the crop. It's His cotton anyway," Hassan said with a smile.

"You'll be sorry!" others called after them, but Adamu and Hassan paid them no mind.

At church the two leaders led the congregation in prayer and thanksgiving for the blessings of the cotton crop. They rejoiced that most of the other Adventist cotton farmers were in church with them. "God is so good," they all sang. After the singing, Adamu preached a message that reminded everyone how much they owed God. "'The earth is the Lord's, and the fulness thereof; the world, and they that dwell therein,'" he read from Psalm 24:1 in the King James Version.

All that day the Adventist farmers' fields were empty of workers as the members prayed and sang and testified of the Lord's goodness in their little concrete-block church. And all that day it did not rain.

The next morning Adamu and Hassan were back in their fields picking cotton, none the worse for the delay. It took them another full day to pick the field clean. It was a good feeling when the long straight rows were stripped of the chalky puffs of white. By Wednesday of that week they had finished separating the seeds from the cotton, and everything was tied up in large bales.

At prayer meeting that night they all praised God for His goodness in helping them harvest their cotton. The service was a simple one, but never were songs sung more lively or prayers prayed more fervently. God had blessed them abundantly, and Adamu knew that honoring God's holy day was part of the reason for this.

They all went home that night and slept the sweet sleep of bliss that God gives to those who do an honest day's work. Adamu and his fellow members had honored God's Sabbath, and He had blessed them for it.

But Satan was not happy. Togo was the evil one's territory, a stronghold of animistic spirit worship, and the last thing he needed was for God's faithful followers to become grounded in the timeless truth of God's holy Sabbath. Now more than ever he began scheming how he could make them pay for their courage. Adamu, Hassan, and the others could not see into the future or fathom the real test of faith that was soon to come.

The next week a government agricultural representative came to town to announce arrangements for the purchase and transport of everyone's cotton. Adamu and Hassan and the other cotton farmers in the village met with the purchasing agent at the town square and learned the details of when and where this would take place. The good news was that a big truck was scheduled to arrive in about 10 days on November 21. The bad news was that when Adamu and Hassan heard the date of arrival, they realized that November 21 was a Sabbath, and for them that could only mean trouble.

The Adventists wouldn't be able to do business with the government on the Sabbath. That was God's holy day, and they must honor it. But if they didn't sell their cotton to the agent when the truck came, they would probably have to wait months until another truck came by again. And that would be a potential financial disaster! As it was, they were poor farmers, hardly able to make ends meet from one harvest to another. There was never enough money to cover the simple costs of life!

That night around the evening fires Adamu and Hassan talked about their options. They could grow most of the food they needed, but farmers always need new tools to replace broken ones, and they had to have extra cash around for medicine and other family emergencies. And if there was a death in the family, besides being an emotional strain, such an event would be a financial one as well. Funerals could be a huge expense, costing thousands of CFA.

But the greatest immediate financial need involved their children. Children had to go to school, or at least they should, and that meant they needed shoes and school uniforms. If there wasn't enough money to go around, some of the children would have to stay home. It was not mandatory for children to attend school, and there was no such thing as free education. Under these circumstances only the eldest son would likely go to school, and Adamu hated the thought that his other children would have no chance at an education during that time. If the next harvest was a good one, they might be able to go back to school again, but they would surely fall behind after missing so many months of school.

As Adamu and Hassan mulled over all these thoughts, they knew there was only one real option—they had to honor the Sabbath. They were confident in their decision about what they should do, but it was the other church members they were worried about.

The two men decided to call an emergency prayer meeting that night. There were 18 families in the church who were cotton farmers, so they called everybody together to discuss the news about the arrival of the government trucks on Sabbath. The two leaders knew there was much at stake. If they did not meet the truck on November 21, they would not be able to sell their cotton. If they did meet the truck, they would be violating their promise to keep God's Sabbath day holy.

"Can't we just have someone else sell our cotton for us?" an old farmer at the meeting asked as the group brainstormed solutions to this quandary they now found themselves in. The shriveled wrinkles of his weather-beaten face showed the tug-of-war going on in his heart.

"That is not an option according to the Bible," Adamu said. "We're not to work, nor are we to have anyone doing work for us. Not our children or animals, and especially not our friends and neighbors. The Sabbath is God's holy day for everyone. Just because our friends and neighbors don't happen to share our convictions doesn't mean they don't owe God their allegiance and worship. If we ask them to sell our cotton for us, we would be as guilty as if we had sold it ourselves."

The members debated the issue for several hours, some making one point, and some another. Hassan stood up and reminded everyone of the stories in the Bible in which God blessed those who honored the Sabbath. "Remember the miracle of the manna in the wilderness?" he asked, glancing from one church member to the next. "That is a perfect example of what God can and will do for us if we obey Him. The people in the desert had very little to eat, but each day manna came. And when Friday came they were told to gather twice as much so they wouldn't have to work at all on

Sabbath morning. And those who did try to gather manna on the Sabbath found none. Six days a week God gave the supply, but on Sabbath there was no manna. This was no accident. For almost 40 years God performed this miracle as a reminder that He would always provide for them. Through this one act, God showed them how much He cared about them." Hassan let his words sink in. "Do you think He cares less about us than them?"

No one could argue his point. Finally Adamu told everyone he thought they should give the decision some more thought. "Let's go home and pray about it for the next two days," he advised. "I think you all know this could be a wonderful opportunity to witness to the village. Think what a message this would send to our friends and families if we take our stand for God and remain faithful to the sacredness of the Sabbath hours."

"Think about it and sleep on it," Hassan told the members as they all filed out into the night and headed home. "At the church service this coming Sabbath, we can make our final decision."

Hassan and Adamu knew this was going to be a real struggle for many of the families who were not yet grounded in the faith. No one could really afford to wait for the truck to come again at some undetermined time in the future, and the weak ones were especially susceptible to Satan's temptations. To tempt them to give in would be the devil's greatest triumph!

The two leaders stayed at the church after everyone else left and prayed for those members they felt were most vulnerable. In the end, the decision to sell or not to sell on the Sabbath would become a personal issue. Undoubtedly so. "That's the way it always is with the most serious of salvation issues," Adamu said as he blew out the kerosene lamps in the church.

Chapter 8

When Sabbath came, there was much debate again, and the Sabbath school Bible study was interrupted by the arguments of several members, one against the other. Adamu suggested they come to an afternoon meeting to discuss the pros and cons of the issue. "We should not be using valuable time during our regular services to discuss matters God has already made clear," he warned. This seemed to make sense to everyone, and once again a peaceful calm settled over the congregation as God's presence filled the little church.

During the afternoon the tone of the conversation began to take on a decidedly different turn. It appeared that most of the farmers felt this was an unusual exception. They felt that they should go ahead and do business with the agent. Many of the members who were not farmers took offense to this stance, but the farmers only seemed to grow more adamant.

"It's easy for you to give advice!" they argued. "It's not your family who will go hungry in the months to come! And besides, we're not going to actually be working! All we have to do is sit by the road at the depot and wait for the truck to come. We'll let the agent and his men load the cotton. It will take only a few minutes of our morning, and then we can come to church as usual."

"You make it sound so simple," Hassan continued, "but it never turns out that way. Satan will see to that for sure!"

Adamu once again begged everyone to consider the importance of the Sabbath covenant and the blessings that come when we honor God. Then he prayed for them all and sent them home.

The week flew by, and Adamu busied himself with work on the farm. He and his boys gathered the tough, wiry cotton plants from the field to be burned in small bonfires. This would clear the fields for the planting of the next crop. Adamu had lots of time to think during the day as he worked with his sons, but it did no good. His heart told him trouble was coming for those who chose to be unfaithful. As he sat around the evening fire with his family, he reminded his children about the importance of being true to God. He knew the biggest lesson of their lives would come the next

Sabbath, and he wanted them to be ready for it. He wanted it to be crystal clear why they were not going to be at the depot with the other farmers waiting to sell their cotton bales to the government agent.

And so he told them all their favorite Bible stories about people who stood for God under persecution and even the threat of death. There were tales about Joseph and David and Daniel and the three boys in the fiery furnace. He had told these stories to them a hundred times before, but this time it was different. This time he was helping his children see the connection between the Bible characters and the test of faith that was soon to come upon them all. Faithfulness under fire would no longer be a concept they just talked about. It would become a reality of life.

Friday evening arrived with the setting of the hot African sun. "I feel a burden for the other cotton farmers like nothing I've ever felt before," he confessed when the evening meal was over and he and Lantana were outside basking in the warm afterglow of a rose-tinted sunset.

"I can tell." She glanced at him with a look that only a wife can give. "You've had worry lines on your face all week, and I know it's not because of our decision to honor God's holy Sabbath."

Adamu smiled, but said nothing in return. It was as if she could read his mind.

"Why don't you spend some extra time in prayer for them tonight?" she added. "Who knows? Maybe you can help turn back the tide of temptation sent upon them by old Mr. Devil."

Adamu had to smile at Lantana. From the day he married this woman he had loved her more than anything, but now after 11 years of marriage he loved her even more. Other men might see their wives as good only for working or having children, but not Adamu. He knew the true value of a godly wife. Lantana was a good mother and a faithful member in their local church, and she always offered words of wisdom when they were needed the most.

And so it was that after the others had all gone to bed Adamu stayed up and prayed. In fact, he spent most of the night in prayer along the forest's edge near a little campfire he built using a few remaining cotton stalks lying around. But even as he prayed for his fellow church members, he couldn't shake the feelings he had about the coming day.

The next morning Adamu didn't eat breakfast. He wanted his mind to be clear for the showdown that was sure to come. Either his fellow church members would be faithful to their convictions to honor the Sabbath, or they would not. Whatever the outcome, it would be an individual decision. The question that plagued his mind was how many would come through for God.

As Adamu headed to town with his family, he was joined by Hassan and his family. They greeted one another with a "happy Sabbath," but it was obvious there was a lot of tension in the air. What would they find when they reached the little Adventist church at the edge of town? Would they discover that everyone had decided to be faithful and come to church after all, or would there be only a few? Even worse, what if none of the other farmers showed up? Adamu and Hassan didn't want to think about that. Of the 18 families who farmed cotton in the area surrounding Toboni, surely some of them would come, wouldn't they?

"Let's sing a song!" Adamu finally said, trying to still his nagging doubts. "This is the Lord's day, and we need to praise Him for it!"

"Amen!" Hassan half shouted as the two families continued on up the dusty African road to town. And so they sang, and the cheerful tunes seemed to do the trick. "Let us sing a song that will cheer us by the way! In a little while we're going home; for the night will end in the everlasting day, in a little while we're going home."

They didn't see any of the other Adventist cotton farmers walking the road to church all dressed up in their best. However, they didn't see them with their carts on the way to the depot either, which they felt was a good sign.

In no time at all they were at the church, and what they found was a mixed blessing for the two church leaders. A few members were already at the church, but none of the other cotton farmers were there yet. However, within a few minutes Bahija and his family arrived to celebrate the Sabbath with them. By now Bahija had a plot of land himself and had planted a few hectares of cotton.

"Praise the Lord!" Adamu said, raising his hand to heaven. "Bahija is here! A man faithful to his God, willing to trust his business to the Creator of heaven and earth! Come, brother, we'll honor the Sabbath together and let God take care of our cotton!"

"Yes, we will!" Bahija echoed. "I don't care what anyone else does, Adamu! Since you introduced me to Jesus and the Bible, my life has never been the same. The blessings I enjoy, just in peace of mind alone, are worth all the sacrifices I might have to make." And then his tone changed as they all sat down together to begin the Sabbath school service. "Where are all the other cotton farmers?" he asked.

"I don't know," Adamu said with a sigh. "We had been hoping against hope that more would take their stand. Maybe they will still come. Did you see any of them on your way to church?"

"Not many," the little man frowned. "I live on this side of town, so that may be it. Most of the others live east and south of town. I did see Marcel and his son pushing their handcart loaded with a bale of cotton. They were heading for the depot along the road where the truck is scheduled to load the cotton. They wouldn't look at me when I greeted them. I think the Lord has probably smitten their consciences quite severely this morning."

"Let's hope so," Adamu replied. "At least they may learn a lesson here, but it's a shame it has to be at such a high cost. They are definitely going to miss a chance to witness for God and show everyone what a blessing God's holy day can be. And worst of all, they're going to miss out on coming to worship in the Lord's house. But you know, I have a feeling it's going to take them longer to do business with the agent than they thought."

"Well, then, let us begin with Sabbath school," Hassan said cheerfully. At that moment two more farming families walked into the church. "Praise the Lord!" Adamu and Hassan jumped to their feet again. Another two victories for God! Now we are five strong!"

"We have all been praying for the cotton farmers in our church," Adamu said as he glanced around at the other merchants and tradesmen in the congregation who had come to worship as usual. "Our prayers have not been in vain. Five families have passed the test of faithfulness and devotion to God's Sabbath. Let's keep praying and singing. Maybe God will bring us more."

Chapter 9

A nd so they began to sing hymns. "'There's a land that is fairer than day, and by faith we can see it afar; for the Father waits over the way, to prepare us a dwelling place there.'" They sang with such passion and energy that Adamu felt himself shivering with inspiration, although the morning was warmer than usual. They sang "Trust and Obey" and "'Tis So Sweet to Trust in Jesus" and then one of Adamu's favorites: "Take My Life and Let It Be!" But no more cotton farmers came.

Then they started the Sabbath school lesson, and Hassan led out in a discussion about the Sermon on the Mount. One set of verses especially made an impact on the group gathered there that morning. "Therefore do not worry, saying, 'What shall we eat?' or 'What shall we drink?' or 'What shall we wear?'" Hassan read from his Bible. "'For after all these things the Gentiles seek. For your heavenly Father knows that you need all these things. But seek first the kingdom of God and His righteousness, and all these things shall be added to you" (Matthew 6:31-33).

Midmorning came and went, and still the other cotton farmers did not come. Adamu leaned toward his wife and whispered, "I wonder what's happened? What can be taking them so long to finish their business with the government agent?" But she could only shake her head at this sad turn of events in a church that had been faithfully honoring God for so many years.

Meanwhile, down at the depot along the road to town the cotton farmers of the community had assembled, toting their handcarts with the heavy cotton bales strapped to them. It was a day of celebration for the village, and spirits were high. They all greeted one another cheerily as they anticipated the day ahead. Today they would sell their cotton for a good price. Today they would reap the rewards of their hard work.

The Adventist farmers among them were unusually quiet. They greeted one another politely, but they said little more than was necessary. It was clear to see by the looks on their faces that they wanted this exchange to be over quickly. Every moment away from the church was a prick to their consciences, a reminder that their religious convictions no doubt meant very little to them. They didn't want to admit it, but they knew they were weak in spirit. Their faith was feeble, and nothing Adamu or Hassan or any of the others had said to encourage them had been able to make them strong. No arguments favoring the Sabbath had dissuaded them from showing up to wait for the truck.

The morning passed, and they could imagine their fellow members up the road singing the familiar hymns of worship. They could see Hassan leading out in the Sabbath school Bible study and Adamu leading out in worship. But it was all wasted on them because they weren't at the church to take part.

Noon came and went. The faithful members in the little church finished the worship hour and sang their final hymn. "Lift up the trumpet, and loud let it ring! Jesus is coming again!" The words rang loud and clear—even the children sang it at the top of their lungs. Then they all filed out and shook hands in a circle as usual before heading home for the Sabbath afternoon meal. The little streets of Toboni were busy as usual on a Saturday, but still the truck had not come.

Merchants and vendors greeted Adamu, Hassan, and their families along the way home. "Why aren't you at the depot waiting for the truck?" the townspeople asked. "Don't you want to sell your cotton?" Many in the streets had heard the rumors about the Adventists who insisted on worshipping God instead of going to the depot.

Adamu smiled at each as they passed. "This is the Lord's day," he told them. "We never do business on the Lord's day."

"But you'll miss the truck," they argued. "If you don't sell your cotton, what will you do for money? You'll have to wait months for the truck to come again."

"Then we'll wait," Adamu nodded. "It's the least we can do for Jesus, who died for us. God has asked that we not work on His holy day, and we will honor His command. God has always provided for our needs, and He won't fail us now."

Most of the vendors could only raise their eyebrows at Adamu's logic. Some even shook their heads in disgust. "God helps those who help themselves," Adamu heard one old grandma mutter. Working hard and providing for your family was the sensible and respectable thing to do in Toboni, and Adamu was very much aware of it. To intentionally avoid meeting the truck was unforgivable in their minds, but Adamu held his head high and only smiled in return. Things might not be exactly as he wished, but he was confident of his stand. He was sure that in the end God would overrule on behalf of the five cotton farmers who had remained faithful to His holy Sabbath. God would care for their families as He had promised.

At the depot the cotton farmers continued waiting in the hot sun, sweating and fanning themselves in the oppressive heat. By now everyone was wondering what could be keeping the truck so long. But the hot sun was the last thing the Adventist farmers were thinking about. And the fact that the truck was late was of little consequence to them now. They had missed a Sabbath's day blessing in the little Adventist church, and it pained them deeply that they had made this decision so easily. Some of them, too easily. In fact, when they thought about it, most had to admit they hadn't even really prayed about their decision to show up at the depot with their cotton instead of attending church.

And small wonder. If they had prayed to God, what exactly would they have expected Him to say? What impressions could they have received as to whether or not they should take their cotton to the loading depot? They already knew the answer to such foolish questions. They had enough light on the matter, and they now knew how it felt to ignore the voice of God. Now more than anything they wished they had listened to Adamu and Hassan and stepped out in faith as they had been urged to do.

The sun was stiflingly hot, and the biting flies buzzed incessantly around the men waiting at the depot. Some of the Adventist farmers began to wonder if they should just take their cotton and go home. Maybe the truck wasn't coming after all. Maybe it wasn't too late to take a stand for God. Thus they reasoned in their hearts, but for all the wrong reasons, and when we argue with such feeble lines, the devil will certainly find a willing heart to follow him just a bit further.

Why would you leave? Satan whispered in their minds. *If you go, what will everyone say here at the depot? The truck will be here any minute. You've waited this long and missed church because of it. Why not stay as long as it takes now?*

And so they stayed, once again convinced against their good judgment, but they were very disappointed at how the day had turned out. Their convictions were now clearly scolding them for not taking their stand to honor God's Sabbath. And still they waited.

Midafternoon came and went. By now some of the farmers sought shelter from the scorching sun in the shade of trees near the road. Some ate rice and pâtés that they bought from vendors who were hawking their wares up and down the street. Some played Kalah, a game that used palm nuts as tokens. Some stretched out to catch an afternoon nap.

And then suddenly, out of the blue, the most unexpected thing happened. It rained. At exactly 4:00 p.m. a thunderstorm hit the village of Toboni with almost no warning. The blue-gray sky quickly grew dark as a stiff wind picked up. Everyone looked at the clouds overhead and talked of getting their cotton under cover, but no one guessed they had so little time in which to do it. Before they could get the huge bales of cotton under cover, the sky opened up as a floodgate.

And how it poured! The rain came down in buckets, dousing everything in sight, including their cotton. This was a disaster! Everyone scrambled, pushing and pulling their carts through what had been dusty streets, but were now fast becoming seas of mud. But it was too little, too late. The precious cotton they had worked so hard to produce was drenched.

Within minutes the sun came out once again, smiling on the devastated farmers as though nothing momentous had happened. But in the glow of the bright afternoon sunlight there was no escaping the truth. Few had managed to get their bales under cover, and no one had thought to bring a tarp to cover the cotton in the event such a disaster should occur. After all, they had been promised the agent would show up first thing in the morning, and that meant they need concern themselves with only sunny skies and a short time of exposure in the open air.

But the day had dragged on, and each time they had heard a truck coming they were sure it would be the agent. And of course they had been disappointed each time. Now all they could do was stare at their cotton, destroyed by a sudden rainstorm.

Chapter 10

The nightmare of every farmer who had ever grown cotton was a reality! After months of hard work planting, cultivating, and harvesting the cotton, it was ruined. Their precious cotton, which could have brought a healthy price on the market, was matted and soggy now, spattered with the hideous red-brown clay of the muddy streets. The farmers had expected a good price, but now they would get little, if anything, for what was left of it, if the agent ever showed up at all.

They tried opening up the bales to air them out and dry the cotton, but it was no use. The cotton was a dripping, saturated, sodden mess! Everyone hung their heads in despair.

And the Adventist farmers were the most devastated of all. If they had not skipped church to bring their bales of cotton to the depot, this would have never happened! If they had been faithful to God and obeyed His commandment as they were supposed to, their cotton would still be safe and dry! They had sat out in the hot sun all day, missing the blessings of church and the knowledge that they were right before God! Even worse, they had failed to be witnesses for God in the little village of Toboni. They had failed to honor the Sabbath, which has been a sign between God and His people throughout the ages. And still the truck hadn't come. What a disaster of a day! How they wished now they had listened to their brothers and sisters at the church!

The shadows were growing long now as the bright yellow sun turned amber and orange and then red. Its fat bulging orb settled lower on the western horizon as though it too was weary from the long, hard day. By now all the farmers were sure the truck would not come. Completely disheartened, they headed home, taking their rain-soaked cotton with them. As they pushed their handcarts along the mud-filled streets, they could only wonder what had become of the purchasing agent and his truck. Had he gotten lost? Had he bypassed them completely on his circuit through northern Togo? Would he choose another day to come and buy their cotton?

But none of these explanations was of any comfort to the Adventist farmers with their guilty consciences. It seemed nothing could make them feel better. They had failed to keep God's Sabbath day holy, and the cotton they had worked so many months to produce was ruined besides.

Obviously some of their fellow members had not come to the depot to await the government truck. Adamu and Hassan for sure. They had been the ones most adamant about not treating God's holy Sabbath as a regular workday. Besides that, it appeared that Bahija, Komi, and Antoine had also remained faithful to the challenge. None of them had been at the depot.

Many of the disheartened famers had to pass by the Adventist church on their way home. By that time it was really getting dark, but they could see lights in the church and could hear the members singing. The Sabbath evening vespers was still going on. Again, they felt pangs of regret that they had spent their day doing something that now seemed so sacrilegious. They had missed a blessing by not keeping the Sabbath. They had chosen to wait for the cotton truck all day, which in the end never did arrive!

What the disappointed Adventist farmers didn't know was that during the afternoon the faithful members had come back to the church again. After more songs and a short Bible study, they had spent the greater part of the afternoon praying for their fellow members who were waiting out by the road with their cotton. Sending their prayers heavenward, they asked that God would continue working on the hearts of those members who had ignored the counsel of the Holy Spirit. With fervent hearts they had prayed that God might still somehow be glorified through this sad story of unfaithfulness.

The forlorn farmers with their loads of cotton could have stopped at the church right then and gained even a small blessing by finishing out their day in God's presence, but they didn't. The thought of having to face their fellow church members and swallow their pride was too much for them to bear. What would Adamu and Hassan say? What would all the other church members say? By now everyone in Toboni knew that a thunderstorm had come up suddenly and ruined the farmers' precious cotton! There would be no end to the shame they would all bear once they again stood before their fellow believers.

And then another thought suddenly struck them. Adamu and Hassan and the other three Adventist farmers who had not shown up still had their cotton under cover. Their cotton was dry and safe and ready to be delivered to the cotton agent when he arrived. What an epiphany, and the irony of it all struck them like a bolt of lightning!

And so they slunk on past the church, hoping their squeaking handcarts wouldn't betray them to the worshippers inside. But they needn't have worried. The faithful members inside were busy singing songs of praise and giving thankful testimonies for a day well spent in the house of the Lord. And yes, they were praying for their brothers who had dared to doubt God's goodness by desecrating His holy day.

It was hardly light the next morning when pounding footsteps could be heard running through the village. "The cotton truck has come! The cotton truck has come!" a boy shouted as he raced on out the country road to spread the good tidings to the farmers.

To the cotton farmers in the village who had been at the depot the previous day, this news was painful. They had patiently waited for the truck all day Saturday, and now they had nothing to show for it.

But it was the unfaithful Adventist cotton farmers who were hurting the most. They had taken the biggest spiritual gamble of their lives and lost. And now, like the disciples after the crucifixion of Jesus, they remained in hiding, afraid to show their faces, afraid to be shamed beyond what their losses had already cost them.

Not surprisingly the messenger boy headed straight for Adamu's house. Everyone in town knew Adamu was the leader of the small group of Adventists who had refused to go to the depot on Saturday to sell their cotton. He and his fellow members had acted like "fools," refusing to do the sensible thing. The cotton truck probably wouldn't return for another six months, everyone had told them, and still they had gone to church, ignoring the warnings of their neighbors. They had remained steadfast and stubborn in their desire to honor God's holy Sabbath day.

The village grapevine had spread the news that Adamu and a few Adventist cotton farmers had spent the day in church singing and praying and studying their Bibles. It was no secret now that they loved their Sabbath, as they called it. In fact, it was clear now that it meant more to them than even the cash they would receive for selling their cotton! This was a concept the villagers did not understand at all.

But now, strangely enough, these religious beliefs were the very thing that had saved the Sabbathkeepers from the financial disaster so recently come upon the town. Not so with the rest of the villagers. No cotton sales meant no new influx of money into the local economy. This of course meant there would be little money to buy shoes and books and school uniforms for the children. There would be no medicine for the sick and the elderly. And of course there would be even less to buy colorful fabric to makes dresses for the wives, or little extras such as dried fish or chocolate for them to enjoy on feast days.

"This strange business of worshipping on Saturday must have something to it!" some village folks muttered as they pondered this stroke of fortune for the Sabbathkeepers. "Could it be that something as simple as the day on which one worships might bring blessings from heaven?"

Chapter 11

T he cotton truck has come, Mr. Adamu!" the messenger boy shouted when he arrived at Adamu's house. "It's here now at the depot!" and he raced off to tell the other farmers in the area.

Adamu was already up eating his breakfast of kokonte and pâté when he heard the news. "Come, Sena and Lucien!" he called to his two sons. "Let's go collect the blessings God has been keeping in store for us!"

The boys ran to the shed and opened the door where two handcarts were already loaded with the huge bales of cotton. "Nice and clean and bright!" Adamu smiled at the cotton radiantly white in the morning sunlight just coming over the golden hills to the east. "We honored the Sabbath, and now God is rewarding us for our faithfulness. Let's get this cotton to market, boys!"

He didn't have to tell them twice. Sena, the older of the two, grabbed the handles of one of the carts. He was only 10 and struggled to manage the heavy load. "I can do it!" he stammered as Adamu reached for the handcart to steady it.

"All right, then," he smiled at his younger son. "We'll take this one, won't we?"

Lucien smiled a toothy grin. "Yes we will!" he said triumphantly as he helped his father push the handcart out of the shed and down the road. Because the loads were so heavy, it took them half an hour to reach the depot, and when they got there they found Hassan and four other Adventist families ahead of them.

They all greeted one another warmly. This was the way to bring cotton to market—on a day when their consciences could be clear, and God could bless them for their efforts.

Adamu arrived at the depot in time to hear the government agent apologizing to the waiting farmers. The man was a Muslim with a Lebanese accent and a white turban on his head. "I'm sorry I'm late," he said as he opened up the back gate of the rack on the truck. "My truck had three flat tires yesterday. The first one I fixed easily enough, because I was still in town at the hotel where I stayed for the night. I did have a bit of a time getting the lug nuts off the front tire, but a mechanic in town helped me. That was at 6:00 in the morning.

"But then I had a second flat tire, and this time it was way out in the middle of nowhere. And of course my spare tire was the flat one I had taken off just that morning, so I had to walk to town to get it fixed. It took me more than two hours to reach town, and then there was no one anywhere in town who could come back out to the truck to help me fix it. So I had to catch a ride to another town, where I finally got someone to come with me to fix the tire.

"By that time it was past noon, and I knew I was going to have to hurry." The agent rolled his eyes and stopped his explanation long enough to wipe his forehead with a cloth. He was somewhat of a storyteller, and by now he had a captive audience as he continued on with his surprising tale. "I had two other stops to make before my stop here in Toboni, but they were small stops with only a few farmers, and I figured I could still make it here well before dark. I hurried along the country roads, but my truck is old, so I always try to be kind to her.

"Anyway, I got out past Sokode a ways to pick up the cotton at Boulabe and Bafilo, and then of all things, would you believe it, I had another flat! The third one that day! I was so angry; I just sat there pounding the steering wheel with my fist! What was going on! I couldn't imagine why I was having so many breakdowns! Never in all the years I've been driving this truck have I ever had more than one flat tire in a day! It was as though Allah was trying to keep me from reaching your village!"

The man glared at the sky as if he really thought God might be behind the delays. "Three flat tires in one day, and you know a truck tire is not an easy thing to change!" Even now the driver seemed baffled by the chain of circumstances. Adamu stood listening to the truck driver's explanation, but he knew in his heart what had happened, and he wasn't really surprised. Just grateful. God in His goodness and providence had found convenient ways to slow things down so that the faithful Adventists in Toboni could sell their cotton on a day other than the Sabbath. After all, Adamu smiled to himself, no one should have to work on the Sabbath. Not even a nonbeliever!

By now dozens of farmers were arriving, pushing and pulling their handcarts loaded with the damaged cotton bales. Many of the Adventists had brought their ruined cotton too, hoping to get at least something for the soggy, red-tinged bundles of cotton on their carts.

As the truck driver finished his story, he glanced around at the downcast faces of the farmers with their pitiful-looking cotton. "What is this?" he demanded roughly. "Why do you bring me cotton of such poor quality? I am not interested in cotton of this sort! Where is the good cotton the people of Toboni always produce?"

The man's words cut deep and stung the pride of the Toboni farmers. Adamu was sure the man didn't know their story, but it wouldn't have made a difference. He was right. Their bales of cotton did look awful! The farmers all hung their heads, but not one offered an explanation.

Finally Adamu stepped forward. "A storm came up suddenly yesterday afternoon, and it rained very hard. Unfortunately the cotton was ruined in the surprise storm."

"Your bad luck is unfortunate." The truck driver squinted at them all in the early-morning sunlight. "But I am not interested in cotton of such poor quality! It's too inferior! Look at it! All soggy and covered with mud!"

He turned to Adamu and Hassan. "You men have bales of high-quality cotton. Are there others without damaged cotton?" Adamu had two large bales, and so did Hassan and Bahija. The other two Adventist farmers who had also missed the rain each had only one. "Did I come all this way for just eight bales?" the truck driver asked unbelievingly.

Adamu shrugged and smiled. "We are small farmers," he admitted. "But as you can see, misfortune has been the lot of many this weekend." The agent softened his tone as he considered the plight of the other villagers, but he sensed a story here too. "Tell me, how is it that you have such clean bales of cotton, while the others have been damaged?"

For a few moments Adamu waited, not knowing quite how to answer. To say the wrong thing just now would be tragic. Not only would it be embarrassing for all the farmers who had ruined their cotton in the rain, but it might also make him appear spiteful or arrogant, at least from their point of view. Adamu knew he and the others with clean cotton were the ones on trial here, and lack of compassion just now would be cruel. One misspoken word, and they would probably be alienated from the village folks for a very long time.

"Well, now," he finally began, "many of us are Seventh-day Adventists and worship God on Saturday. We call it the Sabbath as the Bible teaches because God rested on the seventh day when He created the world. So when we heard that your truck would be arriving on Saturday, we knew we could not bring our cotton, because God has asked us not to work on that day. It is His holy day and we must honor it as the commandment has said. Six days you shall labor, but not on the Sabbath." Adamu paused, but the agent waited quietly as if wanting to hear more. The whole crowd was silent too, listening to the testimony of this godly man among them.

"We five men here and our families did not come yesterday with the others. Instead, we worshipped God at our church as we always do on Saturday mornings." Adamu turned to gesture at Hassan and the others with him. "Almost everyone else came to the depot because they didn't want to miss the opportunity of selling you their cotton. But then the thunderstorm hit quite unexpectedly, and they all got caught in the rain, as you see here by the condition of their cotton."

No one said anything when Adamu finished, but then one of the other Adventist farmers with damaged cotton finally stepped forward. "Adamu's right," he said quite frankly, his eyes on the ground. "And I can tell you one thing for sure. I've learned a valuable lesson this weekend. I did not have the courage to go to church with Adamu and the others yesterday. I was too concerned I might lose the chance to sell my cotton." The man spoke honestly with a touch of sadness in his voice, but he didn't seem angry. "If I had to do it over again, I would side with Adamu and Hassan and go to church as I knew I should. This experience has shamed me as it should."

The driver had been listening intently, and now he finally spoke. "So this is why I had all those flat tires?" He glared at Adamu in mock anger, and then he began to laugh. Others began to laugh too, and all the village men joined in. It felt good to see the townsfolk relaxing once more, and for the first time in Adamu's memory, it felt as though they were a united community.

Then the truck driver loaded Adamu's cotton and all the rest of the clean bales, and paid them a hefty price for it since there was so little cotton in Toboni. He reluctantly offered to buy the mud-soaked cotton, too, but for a mere pittance compared to what they had hoped to get for it. "It's against my better judgment," he admitted. "Let's hope it will be a sign of goodwill between us in the future."

Chapter 12

In the weeks and months that followed, times were hard for Toboni. The loss of the farmers' cash crop was a tragedy they had not expected to have to bear. Cotton was their major source of income, and now they had to wait until the next harvest to recoup their loss.

And for the unfaithful Adventists who had insisted on taking their cotton to the depot that fateful Sabbath, it was a double indemnity. They had lost the needed source of income and the sense of integrity that comes with faithfulness to God. Besides that, they lived with the memory that they had not been true to their convictions and their promise to honor the Sabbath. They had been weak at a crucial moment when the village of Toboni was watching, and had missed the opportunity to witness for Jesus.

But Adamu and Hassan encouraged these disheartened members, never bothering to remind them of their lack of faith. Instead, they assured them of the promise of days to come when God would provide them with other tests of loyalty and love for His cause. "Faithfulness begins here at home," Adamu told them. "Before we can do great things for God we must do small things for Him. The gospel must go to all the world, but it first begins in the hearts of His children here in our own little town in Togo."

In the years that followed, the old men of Toboni recounted around the evening campfires the story of when God came very near to them all. It was a time of testing during which everyone got exactly what they needed. Some had failed to live up to their convictions to honor the Lord's holy Sabbath, and for them God sent a kind but poignant reminder of the importance of obedience. In His goodness He sent a thunderstorm to teach the faithless ones a lesson of integrity and respect for His sacred day.

And for the faithful few who dared to stand for God, there were many blessings. Because they obeyed Him, placing His commandments above all other priorities in their life, He honored them with a clear act of providence. They had risked a half year's wages in their zeal to cherish His Sabbath, and for this He delayed the coming of the cotton truck.

The message was loud and clear for everyone to see, a reminder to everyone that faithfulness to God carries with it consequences of greatest importance. Indeed, honoring the Sabbath brings the promise of spiritual and material blessings, and that is something no one can take away. That is a lesson no one should ever forget.

BEHIND ENEMY LINES

Chapter 1

The sun had risen on the coastal town of Paynesville, Liberia, chasing away the milky shadows of dawn. Emerald cuckoos sang their early-morning sonnets from the tall mahogany trees bordering the creek, and agama lizards raced along the tops of cement-block walls. Day had just begun, and already the humid temperatures of West Africa were pushing 90 degrees. Electrical power in town had been sporadic lately, and brownouts were common, but it wouldn't have made much difference anyway. Only the rich could afford the luxury of air-conditioning. For most folks the feeble fans in the homes of the common people did their best to stir the tepid morning air.

But there were other things to worry about besides the stifling African heat on this July morning. For several months now news had been seeping in from the north and east and west that four armies, each with its own self-appointed revolutionary leader, had been advancing on the capital city of Monrovia. Each army of mercenaries was intent on being the first to capture the city and successfully stage a coup against Samuel Doe, the sitting dictator-president.

And now the revolutionaries had finally arrived. Three days ago a tribal warlord named General Charles Taylor and his guerrillas had poured from the overgrowth of the jungle at the edge of town. Like an army of ants, they entered every street and alley looking for people of the Krahn tribe, and anyone else who might be supportive of the ruling regime of the current government.

The morning was charged with an ominous foreboding of things to come. Not a soul dared venture out. It just wasn't safe. All night long the erratic staccato of machine gunfire had been heard in the streets of Paynesville, but now with the break of day, worse was to come.

Marbu, a young Seventh-day Adventist attending a local college, had risen early with the rest of the town, unable to sleep because of the gunfire. The previous night a stray bullet had come through an open window and struck the wall just above his head. An inch lower and Marbu knew he would have been part of history. "Lord, what will happen to us?" he asked prayerfully as he sat at the kitchen table, his Bible open to his favorite verses of Scripture. "Though an army may encamp against me, my heart shall not fear; though war may rise against me, in this I will be confident" (Ps. 27:3). Right now verses such as this one were the only thing that brought him comfort.

He glanced around the kitchen. There was nothing to eat in the house except a little leftover rice from the night before, but Marbu couldn't bring himself to eat it. He was too worried about what might be coming next. For three days now his family had been holed up here in his brother's house watching and waiting.

"I see you can't sleep either," his brother, Suah, mumbled sleepily as he entered the kitchen.

"You got that right." Marbu rubbed his tired eyes.

"You think it's going to get worse?"

Marbu turned the pages of his Bible. "I'm praying it won't."

Suah stared out the window as he took a long drink of water. "I'm getting tired of all this suspense! We should have left when we saw all those people fleeing south earlier this week." He turned to Marbu again. "When it gets dark tonight, we ought to make a break for it and sneak out of town."

"It's too dangerous!" Marbu argued. "If the revolutionaries catch us on the road, they might force us into their army, or worse—kill us if they think we're out to make trouble." Marbu stared at his Bible. "I say we sit tight and let this whole thing blow over. The revolutionaries will be headed for Monrovia soon. Anyone who goes out in the open right now is crazy!"

Suah yawned. "You've got a point."

A sudden knocking at the door brought Marbu to his feet. *Who could that be at this early hour?* he wondered as he glanced at his brother fearfully. *A neighbor needing help? Another family member? Already there were eight members of the family hiding out in Suah's house. Could it be the government police?* The knock sounded impatient, and Marbu's instincts told him trouble was coming.

"Open it," Suah nodded in the direction of the door. Marbu opened the door to find two military police standing there in full uniform. The commandos had yellow armbands on their sleeves and wore camouflaged army helmets. But the AK-47 assault rifles they held in their hands were what really scared Marbu. Just three feet away from him were the muzzles of guns that could kill him in a heartbeat. He stifled a surge of panic rising inside of him.

"You folks are going to have to come with us!" one of the commandos barked.

"Why?" Marbu stared at the soldiers. "What have we done?"

"We'll see!" the soldier's eyes narrowed. "For now we've got orders to send everybody over to that open field on the other side of the creek." He pointed west. "How many people are here in the house?"

Marbu stared at the two commandos, hoping this was all a bad dream. "Nine," he finally heard himself stammer. "When do we have to go?"

"Right now!" one of the commandos growled. "Everyone in town has to go to the checkpoint! Cross the creek and head straight to the checkpoint opposite the general store! You'll find soldiers waiting for you there! They'll take your identities when you arrive! We're headed that way ourselves, so leave everything and come with us now!"

Marbu couldn't believe this was happening. These soldiers obviously meant business, but what did they really want? Was this some kind of trap? Were they going to loot the house after everyone left?

Suah stepped up behind Marbu. "OK, just give us a minute!" he replied, trying not to anger the soldiers.

"Hurry it up! We don't have all day!" the commandos shouted.

Marbu stared at the two soldiers as they moved on to the next house. "Are they serious?" he muttered to Suah. "Is this some kind of drill?"

"You'd better believe they're serious!" his older brother frowned. "Drill or not, they're not playing games here!"

Marbu hoped he would wake up and discover this was just a nightmare. What was happening? This was Liberia, one of the best spots to live in West Africa. Liberia was a free democratic nation that had good government relations with the United States. There had been attempted coupes and rumors of war during the previous few years, but things always smoothed themselves out in the end. How could this whole thing be happening? How could soldiers come and treat everyone like this?

"What do you think they're going to do with us?" Marbu grabbed his brother by the arm.

"I have no idea, but we'd better hurry!" Suah clapped his hands together to wake up the family. "All right, everybody! It's time to get up! We've got to go out for a while! Get up!"

The family members sat up sleepily, their minds in a fog. There was Suah's wife, Monji, and his three children, plus James, the third brother in the family, and a nephew with his girlfriend who had come for a visit.

Suah turned to his wife who was finally awake. "Monji! We must hurry! Get the kids up! We've got to go into town!"

"Why? What's happening?"

"Soldiers have come and told us to go to the athletic field across the creek!"

"What do the soldiers want?" She looked as white as a sheet.

"Can't really say." Suah pulled his 3-year-old son from a mat on the floor and began dressing him. "It appears they want to see our identities. We'd better get our papers and take them with us. Must have something to do with the war north and west of here."

"Well, why didn't they just ask to see our identity papers here at the house?" Monji demanded, her voice rising to a whining pitch.

"I don't know, Monji!" Suah snapped. "They didn't tell us why! Just get the kids ready now! Stop asking so many questions! The man said to hurry! I don't want him to think we're stalling!"

Chapter 2

Marbu helped his little niece get dressed. By the time he finished, the others were all waiting at the door, but the younger ones kept fretting about having to get up so early. "Come on, kids," Marbu said as he knelt on the floor beside them and tried to cheer them up with a smile. "We get to go over to the general store. Maybe we can buy some candy!" He wanted to be brave for the kids, but inside he was shaking like a leaf. This whole thing looked like one of the typical police raids he had heard about, but he had never experienced such an event. His head told him everything would be all right, but his heart told him worse was coming.

Marbu was the last one to leave the house, so he closed the door and locked it behind him. He wanted to protect what few belongings they had in the house, but he realized if anyone wanted to break in while the family was gone, they'd have very little trouble.

And that was entirely possible. Marbu had heard of raids like this being run on unsuspecting citizens who were powerless to do anything about it. The police would conveniently send the family away on some goose chase, wait until they were out of range, and then come back to break the door down. The door to Marbu's brother's house was made of solid wood, but the hinges were weak and could easily be broken with a running kick or maybe a piece of pipe.

The family hurried to the creek behind the house and began wading across as the soldiers had ordered. Four folks from next door crossed with them. Marbu stared at the water swirling around them as the group pushed their way through the current, and his mind wandered to childhood memories of playing in Old Creek, as they called it. He and his friends had caught frogs there. And they had fished in it and swam in it on hot, humid days. Those days seemed so far away now! As he climbed the creek bank on the other side, his heart was racing! He could feel the cool water running out of his trousers and shoes. He could smell gunpowder. He could taste salty sweat running down his face and onto his lips. Clearly this was no dream. It was a real-life nightmare!

What will we be expected to do at the checkpoint? he wondered. *Provide*

ID? Offer proof of our tribal origin? His mind was in a whirl, but he had no answers, and he feared the worst. The thought of this identity thing being a tribal affair was a scary one because tribal skirmishes were usually the worst kind. One tribe hated another, and there was little the government or even the church could do about it. When people wanted to hate each other, that was usually what they ended up doing, and a whole train of consequences usually followed. Most of the time there were interrogations and beatings, and sometimes people were killed.

As he left the shelter of the overhanging trees along the creek, he heard bits and pieces of rumors coming from other folks already gathered there. No doubt this operation was being engineered by General Charles Taylor and his army of some 10,000 guerrillas. The revolutionaries seemed to be interested in finding people from the Krahn tribe more than anything else. The Krahns were a tribe who held the majority of power in the government right now, and were said to be in league with the president of Liberia, and very corrupt. Taylor and his cronies wanted Doe out. It was as simple as that.

By now Marbu could see hundreds of people streaming toward the checkpoint on the town commons. This was no little security exercise. To make matters worse, soldiers were everywhere, and Marbu heard gunshots again somewhere in the distance. He could hear people screaming across town, and tried not to think about what must be happening to them.

When Marbu and his family arrived across from the general store, they saw long lines of people waiting to be questioned by the uniformed soldiers. Some of the soldiers were seated at tables, shouting orders to the people. Others just stood by as sentries, with AK-47s slung over their shoulders, as they scrutinized everyone in the crowd.

A distinguished officer was in charge of the interrogations, and made sure everyone knew it. "If you value your life, have your identity papers ready when you get to the head of the line!" he barked. Marbu learned the officer's name was Mohammed, one of Charles Taylor's mercenaries. He looked to be from the French-speaking country of Burkina Faso to the north. Or was it Libya, maybe? He had an Arabic accent, and that could mean trouble because the Muslims and Liberians had a history of war and hostile bloodshed.

Mohammed's face was like stone. He looked to be a hard man behind his intimidating sunglasses. He was dressed in a sharp-looking khaki uniform and had a .357 Magnum pistol strapped to his side. The two MPs nearby were no doubt his own personal bodyguard.

Leaving his lower officers to do the actual questioning at the checkpoints, Mohammed walked the line with a cold stare that truly frightened the Africans waiting their turn to be interrogated. He pointed at first one man, and then another, singling them out as suspected members of the Krahn tribe. Anyone from the Krahn tribe was a potential enemy and thereby worthy of death.

Other tribes—the Bassa people, the Mende, and the Gio—lived in southern Liberia near the capital, but that didn't seem to concern Mohammed. His only wish was to eradicate as many of the Krahn people as possible. With a mere gesture he ordered the victims to be dragged off, begging and pleading for their lives. Then he moved on down the line.

Were these people being hauled away to die? Marbu wondered. Cries for mercy fell on Mohammed's ears as if he were deaf, and like everyone, Marbu cringed at the officer's nasty manner.

"What are you looking at?" Mohammed shouted at one man who dared to make eye contact with him. He struck the man with his fist, knocking him to the ground, and then ordered him sent to the firing squad.

What kind of demon is possessing the soul of this African officer? Marbu tried not to stare at Mohammed. It was clear that life in this small African town was cheap to these mercenaries.

"Don't anybody move," Marbu muttered under his breath to the other family members standing nearby. "Look as inconspicuous as you can." He tried to smile at his brother's children. "Maybe the commander won't notice us if we're quiet," but Marbu feared this might not be enough.

Almost constantly now he could hear the staccato of machine gunfire from the road the hapless victims were being marched down. How many were being killed? Dozens? Hundreds? And what was this senseless, insatiable thirst for blood that gripped Charles Taylor and the soldiers with him? What was it that made them hunt down the Krahn people as if they were animals? They were enemies politically, but how was it that such treacherous animosity existed between the two people groups? What could compel people to live with such hate and go to such lengths to exterminate one another? Evidently, there was much bad blood. Mohammed showed no mercy as he pulled men from the line, even if he only suspected them to be of the Krahn tribe.

"Notice his forehead and cheekbones," Mohammed said of one man who had been brought to him for questioning. "His features betray him!" For others it was something they said that "incriminated" them. "Notice how sympathetic this woman was toward that tall Krahn we just took away. She must be from the Krahn tribe too! Kill her! We can't take any chances!" Mohammed barked the orders easily, as if he and his officers were ordering meat at the village market.

It was a surreal moment for Marbu as he stood watching the dreadful scene before him! Men and women were being removed from the line by the dozens, and even small children could not escape Mohammed's calloused commands. Marbu's heartbeat quickened as he realized just how serious the situation was becoming for him and his family. Papers or not, if Mohammed and his men suspected anyone of being from the Krahn tribe, they were as good as dead. There seemed to be no way of escape!

Chapter 3

Marbu didn't even want to think about how many people Mohammed's men had already killed in Paynesville. He had no idea how many Krahns were living in Paynesville, but he knew thousands had probably fled to the coast to escape Charles Taylor's relentless campaign of genocide. What would happen to them now? Would they all be hunted down like animals and shot? It made Marbu ill just thinking about it. This was all so totally wrong, so terribly, drastically inhuman! He could only wonder how long it would be before this nightmare was over and the soldiers moved on to the next town.

There were hundreds and hundreds of people in the open field now waiting to be identified, but the going was slow. Each family and each person had to produce papers to prove where they were from and which political party they favored. "What's the point?" Suah mumbled under his breath. "I don't care about politics. I'm not even a member of a political party."

The hot morning sun beat down on them mercilessly. Marbu pulled some banana leaves from a banana plant nearby and fashioned hats for the children to keep them cool from the blazing sun. Then he made a hat for himself, but by now he was dehydrated and beginning to feel the effects of exposure to the sun. He had a splitting headache that wouldn't quit.

By noon some of the older folks and little children began to collapse from heat exhaustion. No one was allowed to eat, but finally the guards allowed a man to bring a pickup with a tank of water on it so that the people could get a drink from a large hose on the back. Hundreds of people surged forward and crowded around the back of the truck, pushing and shoving their way as if they were a herd of wild animals. The children cried for water, but Suah kept them from going forward until the crowd had thinned out. Things were so volatile right now; it wasn't worth the risk!

At one point two men began fighting for a spot at the hose, and the soldiers shot into the air with their rifles to break it up. The rest of the crowd pulled back in fear, unsure of what the soldiers might do next.

All afternoon Marbu and his family waited in line to have their identity papers inspected. As the day dragged on, it became evident this was not going to be a clear-cut process. Some folks were dismissed without so much as a look. Maybe the soldiers knew the families, or maybe their facial features just didn't look like folks from the Krahn tribe. Marbu was glad for all the folks who were being sent away to safety. Soon they would be in their homes, where food and water awaited them.

Some in the crowd worked a little too hard trying to convince the soldiers they weren't enemies of Charles Taylor or his allies. These folks were usually interrogated extensively. In fact, it seemed the more people argued with the interrogators, the more they were scrutinized. If they tried to beg or plead their case, the release took longer, and in many cases they were led away sentenced anyway.

Marbu wondered what it was going to take to convince the inspectors he and his family were not enemies of Charles Taylor. They were just common, ordinary folks, not at all interested in this revolutionary campaign.

Finally the big round sun went down in the west, and with it came the cooler temperatures of evening. The weather was still warm, but anything was better than the heat of day. By now everyone was sitting down on the ground. Many, like Marbu, were sick from being in the hot sun all those hours, and most were ravenously hungry. No one had eaten anything all day except the few who had feared the worst and thought to bring some food along. Little children cried pathetically, but there was very little to give them. Any mangoes or papayas that had been hanging around the edges of the field were long gone. Even the green ones. There had been lots of coconuts lying around on the ground too, but by now they had all been cut open for their refreshing coconut milk.

As twilight settled on the town of Paynesville, Marbu had time to take stock of their situation. Hundreds of people had been interrogated at the checkpoint. Many had been cleared and sent back home, but many others had been led away to be shot. And now that it was getting dark, the soldiers knew they would have to post guards everywhere to keep people from escaping into the jungle.

Mohammed's soldiers had ordered the townspeople to gather wood before dark, and now everyone was ordered to build huge bonfires around the borders of the field. Marbu could see the firelight reflected on the shiny black barrels of the soldier's rifles, and he had to wonder what his chances were of escaping even at night. What were the odds that he would be caught and shot if he tried? The thought was a frightening one, but a very real possibility now. So many others had died already, and who knew how many more would have to suffer at the hands of these madmen.

A sudden round of machine gunfire rang out on the evening air, bringing a rash of hysterical screams from the waiting crowd. Everyone flattened themselves on the ground to avoid stray bullets.

"If anyone tries to escape tonight, they'll be shot!" Mohammed shouted from where he stood in the back of his military jeep. His eyes slowly scoped the captive crowd. He would finish the job he had come to do! He would cleanse this town of its Samuel Doe sympathizers.

"We'll be patrolling the perimeter of this field tonight," he added as he surveyed the crowd one last time, and then they drove off into the gathering darkness.

Marbu was glad to see Mohammed go, but it didn't help his stomach any. He hadn't eaten all day, and the craving for food gnawed at him like a hungry rodent. But what could he do? What could any of them do? The soldiers cared little for the needs of the townspeople. All they knew were the orders of their commander, Mohammed, and those of General Charles Taylor. Other than that nothing else seemed to matter.

"Be very quiet," Marbu whispered to the children. "I think the soldiers want this over so they can go on to Monrovia, so we must be patient. The more noise we make, the more likely they'll notice us." He put on his bravest smile and drew Suah's kids close in the darkness.

Marbu hadn't seen any looting going on, and the women had been left alone until now. But under the cover of darkness he knew that could all change quite quickly. War did strange things to soldiers. It made them heartless and cruel and even demonic as they went on their rampages to kill, sometimes indiscriminately.

In the deepening shadows of night with the cheerful chirp of crickets all around, Marbu finally had time to reflect on the day. Now he began to ask himself some serious questions. *Where is God? Does He care what is happening tonight in Paynesville?* Marbu guessed He did. God always cares. *No doubt this whole thing is bringing Him great sadness,* Marbu reasoned. It wasn't His idea to have people running around starting civil wars and killing innocent people. It was Satan's work, the plan of an evil mastermind.

Marbu had seen plenty of evidence of Satan's dark, sadistic footprints in the culture of Liberia's West African villages. There were the drunken parties when beer flowed freely, making men abusive of their wives. There was the gambling of the little bit of money men had on foolish African games such as Abbia and Mancala. And of course there was the dancing and feasting on the cultural holidays when the rites of spiritualistic divination were practiced.

Fear of the evil spirits controlled every aspect of village life—the power they had over the people was incredible! Nothing was done without consulting the witch doctor, or shaman, as the Liberians called him. For most people, every major life decision was passed through his bag of amulets and magic tricks. The local economy ran on this notion, and the gifts people gave the shaman for his blessings or curses were a very real part of village tribal lore. When sickness came, the shaman was consulted for the voodoo he could perform. If the grade for a school exam hung in the balance, the shaman could be consulted.

In the animistic superstitions of West Africa, deceased family members were believed to come back in the form of an animal or bird or reptile. These creatures were honored and even worshipped for their powers. During exam week a dead rooster hung around the neck could bring good marks if that happened to be the family symbol. An offering of food to a green mamba could avert disaster.

But for Liberians the fear of the dead was the worst.

Chapter 4

In the tribal traditions of spiritualistic folklore, those who have gone on before must be given a proper send-off or the consequences could be catastrophic. Not showing up at the funeral of a relative or friend was unthinkable. And to come without a gift was taboo. The belief was that even a bit of food or a scrap of colorful cloth could be laid in the coffin beside the body, lest the deceased return to haunt those who showed little concern.

Marbu squatted with hundreds of others on the grass of the commons and stared at the fires blazing all around the perimeter of the open field. Here and there he could hear the whimpers of children now grown weary with the long wait. The evening air hung heavy with a foggy mist, and families huddled together for comfort.

Darkness had fully come now with no trace of the royal blue horizon in the west. On the equator the sun sets fast, and when it does the blackness of night comes in a hurry. Marbu sat watching the sparks from the fires dance and shiver above the infernos, as they sailed in zigzag patterns up into the night. Out in the darkness beyond the fires, he could see soldiers lighting up cigarettes now and then. The surrounding jungle seemed quite peaceable with its chorus of crickets and the twitter of night birds now and then.

But Marbu knew this backdrop was anything but peaceful. There was nothing to eat, and although they had managed to get a drink of water from the water truck, the elements of the equator had taken their toll on the waiting crowd. Sad eyes and windblown hair gave everyone a desperate look. Most wanted to believe this whole nightmare would somehow end if they could just go to sleep.

His mind was full of questions about what would come with the morning light. *Will the soldiers finally let us go, or is it only going to get worse?* he wondered. There was a method in the madness of these revolutionaries. They had an objective. If all the rumors about Charles Taylor were true, heads would roll for those who had sympathized with the tribal Krahns now holding power in the government capital.

Then again, maybe Samuel Doe would surprise everyone. Maybe the tide would turn as his military forces fanned out from Monrovia, putting the rebel bands to flight. One could hope.

Marbu searched for an empty space to lie down on the ground. Where would he sleep? Where would anyone sleep? The ground wasn't a safe place to be at night with snakes and scorpions everywhere. Add to that the biting, malaria-infested mosquitoes, and the odds were frightening indeed.

By now many folks had laid themselves out on the hard ground and were fast asleep in spite of the dangers. The one safeguard they seemed to take was to prop their heads up on their elbows, as Africans often do to keep bugs from crawling into their ears.

But Marbu couldn't sleep. He sat down on the ground and pulled his knees close. *Please Lord,* he prayed, staring up at the velvety blackness of the night sky. *Our situation is desperate! Help us! You are all-powerful. We have nowhere to turn but You. We don't know what these soldiers are planning to do, and we're afraid. Satan has his armies doing his bidding here tonight, but we know You rule the world.*

His conversation with God gave Marbu some assurance, though he had to keep reminding himself of it. *"God is our . . . very present help in trouble."* He replayed a familiar passage of Scripture in his mind. *"Therefore we will not fear, even though the earth be removed, and though the mountains be carried into the midst of the sea"* (Ps. 46:1, 2). That's what God was all about, and if ever Marbu needed help, it was now. They all needed it. Suah, Monji, Suah's three children, and the other family members all huddled tightly together.

Marbu tried to sleep, but rest didn't come easy. Not sitting up, and not with all these mosquitoes. He finally dozed off, but he drifted in and out of an uneasy sleep all night.

Sometime before dawn Marbu stirred, but he had a heavy feeling in his chest. The day was fast approaching with no relief in sight. The fires had burned low now, and for hours Marbu had seen no cigarettes light up. The guards were most likely sleeping. If he and his brothers wanted to make a plan, they needed to do it now.

Who knew what the new day would bring? They couldn't hope to escape, not the whole family anyway. But if they didn't get some food for the kids, and more water, things would definitely get worse. How much whimpering and complaining from the kids would Taylor's solders tolerate? They had looked a bit too trigger-happy the day before, and neither Marbu nor Suah wanted to give them reasons to get crazy.

Suah was awake now too, and he was more than willing to plan a strategy with Marbu. A whispered conference between the two of them brought a temporary solution. They would sneak back across the creek to the house to get some food and whatever else they could bring. It was a calculated risk, but one they were willing to take. They had no other options.

Quietly, stealthily, they walked on their hands and feet, as their uncle had taught them to do when on a hunt. Being careful not to scuffle the sand and twigs beneath their feet, they picked their way through the sleeping crowd sprawled on the open ground. Not until they reached the creek 200 yards away did they dare to whisper to each other as they crossed the swift-flowing waterway.

When they reached the house, they found it had not been broken into yet. There had been no looting. Probably the soldiers had been too busy to think about ransacking any of the homes in the neighborhood.

The two men stepped into the darkness of the house and stopped to catch their breath. Then they collected what food they could find. Some mangoes and papayas. Some cooked manioc and sweet potatoes and bread. Two plastic jugs of water, each holding one gallon of precious water. As an afterthought they grabbed some shirts and an extra set of clothes for the kids. Who knew how much longer they would be out on the commons waiting to be cleared.

It was all done in less than five minutes, and then they were returning across the creek again. Carefully they skirted the edge of the field strewn with sleeping bodies to find their way to the family. Twice Marbu's heart nearly leaped into his throat when a child cried out and an old man snored loudly. But no one stirred among the guards, and soon they were back again beside James, Monji, and the others.

Dawn finally came. Everyone stumbled stiffly to their feet. People were grouchy and hungry, wishing for even a morsel of food. They had had enough of the hard ground and the biting mosquitoes, but now came the intense heat of another day.

All morning Marbu and his family waited in line to be interrogated by Mohammed and his officers. Suah made an umbrella-of-sorts with some sticks and the extra shirts they had brought from the house. It wasn't much, but something was better than nothing when it came to protecting the children from the ball of fire above.

Marbu knew his family's identity cards were legitimate, but he was afraid Colonel Mohammed might find reasons to doubt their authenticity. Would he accuse Marbu and his family of being from the Krahn tribe, as he had done with so many folks the day before? Anything might rouse his suspicions. Anything could tip the interrogators in the wrong direction. A word mispronounced. The shape of a cheekbone or forehead. A look in the eye. Would he take them away to be shot? The thought seemed too awful to contemplate, but Marbu had to admit that it was a real possibility.

Already, even at this early hour, dozens of men and women were being singled out and forced to follow MPs who led them off down the road. Some refused to go, kicking and screaming at the soldiers as if that might help. Some of the victims Marbu knew to be of the Krahn tribe, but some were definitely not. All of them begged for mercy, and some cursed Colonel Mohammed, but that only made the soldiers more violent. The end result was always the same.

The muffled sound of distant gunfire could once again be heard through the barricade of jungle foliage, and everyone knew what that meant. Any of them could be next.

Marbu bowed his head and prayed instinctively. *Please, Lord, spare us,* he moaned. *I'm asking for our lives, Lord. That's all. Let the soldiers do what they may, but please, Lord, spare our lives!*

Chapter 5

Marbu stared at the blanched faces of his family members and wondered how much more of this Monji and the children could take. Would they crack under the pressure? Would they break down and get hysterical as others had? Marbu knew he couldn't afford to let that happen. The longer they all waited, the better their situation would be. Sooner or later something would happen to give them a break. For the family to escape into the jungle was out of the question, but there was always the hope that President Doe and his forces would come to Paynesville and rescue them all. It wasn't likely, but there was always that chance.

Noon came and the officers took a break in the shade, but of course there was no relief for the scores of people still standing in line. The water truck came by again, which helped some. They were all famished, but water was the thing they needed most.

Finally about midafternoon Marbu and his family reached the head of the line at the makeshift checkpoint. The commando sitting on the wooden bench behind the interrogation table held out his hand for the family papers. He looked tired. His eyes were bloodshot, and Marbu even found himself feeling just a little bit sorry for the man. Maybe the officer had been doing this for weeks now. Maybe he had grown tired of eating makeshift meals while on the road with the army. Maybe this wasn't even really his war.

Marbu handed him the papers, and the commando set them down on the table and started going through them one by one. He flipped through the pages of the little books as if he had done it a thousand times before, and Marbu guessed that he probably had. The soldier seemed to be in a hurry, though, and Marbu wondered what that might mean.

"How long have you lived in this town?" he asked Suah without looking up from the pages.

"Since I was a boy. My grandfather and father moved here in 1964."

"And how about you?" the officer glanced at Marbu. "What are you doing in town?"

"I'm a student attending classes at the local College of West Africa.

We're brothers." Marbu gestured toward Suah and his other brother, James. "We're from the Bassa tribe here in Paynesville."

Marbu looked calm and collected as he answered the officer's questions one by one, but inside he was shaking like a leaf. One false move, one bad answer, and they could be finished. The officer could pull them from the line just as likely as not. He could order their execution on a mere whim as he had done with so many others.

After much consideration, the officer finally gave them back their papers and waved them on. Colonel Mohammed sat in the shade of a tree and stared at Marbu's family from behind his jaded sunglasses as they gathered up their few belongings to go.

"OK," Suah mumbled under his breath to his family, "let's do this real slowly. Don't anyone move too fast here. Don't get excited. Just walk toward home. We don't want to give the soldiers any reason to call us back."

Home had never seemed so far away as Marbu and the family walked the few hundred yards across the field toward the creek. Finally though, they entered the welcome shade of the creek bottom. The water felt good on their hot faces and tired bodies, and Marbu wanted to shout for joy as he dipped himself into the water. But he remembered Suah's warning and kept walking.

As they all climbed out of the creek on the other side, Marbu had to take a reality check to remember all that had happened during the previous two days. Had it been only a day and a half since the soldiers first ordered them to the checkpoint? Had they really slept out on the town commons the night before? Had he and Suah actually been here at the house this morning in the early shadows of dawn, smuggling food and water back to the family?

None of it seemed real now at all to Marbu, but it didn't really matter. They were free again at last, and that was enough.

Inside the house they put a meal together quickly, but the children wouldn't wait. They simply grabbed whatever they could find and began wolfing it down. "Easy now," Suah cautioned them all. "We've got plenty of time to eat."

No one talked while they took small handfuls of rice with their fingers and dipped them in the spicy peanut sauce. There was bread too and more than enough slivers of papaya from an armload of fruit Suah had just picked behind the house.

After they had eaten their fill, they sat around enjoying the feel of it in their stomachs, but Marbu could tell the wheels in Suah's head were turning. "I don't think we can afford to stay here," he said, voicing the very thoughts Marbu had been having. "We're home now, but I don't trust those soldiers."

Monji got an angry look on her face. "They said we're OK and could go home, didn't they?" Her eyes flashed the same way they had the morning the soldiers ordered them out. It was as though she was irritated at her husband for even suggesting the idea of such a thing. They had just arrived home, hadn't they? Did he really expect her to leave? She was going nowhere!

Marbu stared at her in surprise. Had Monji already forgotten the danger of the ordeal they had just been through? He couldn't believe it! He would have smiled at her little outburst if it hadn't been such a serious situation. She had never been one to really count the cost of any situation, no matter what the dangers were! Her temper always seemed to get the best of her, and here it was again, making her think irrationally.

But Suah would hear none of her complaints. "Now listen to me carefully!" he said firmly in low tones as though he feared he might be overheard. "We have no guarantee those commandos will not be back again. Do you want to run that risk?" He stared at his wife impatiently, as if she were a child. "If they do come back, this time it might be to execute us after all!"

The afternoon sun was sinking lower in the sky now, and streaky shafts of dusty sunshine angled in through the open windows. Marbu glanced around him at the familiar surroundings. He knew what Suah was going to suggest next, and he didn't like it any more than Monji did, but he also realized it might be their only option. He was bone weary from sleeping fitfully on the ground the night before, and he was dehydrated from so much time out in the sun. But Suah was right. They had to go.

"We can stay at my uncle Sundagar's house north of town," Suah finally said. "It's farther away from the checkpoints they've set up here in Paynesville. If things get worse, we can always leave from there." He noticed the crestfallen faces of his children. "Don't worry," he added. "After this whole thing is over, we'll come back. Now gather up what you can and let's go." His voice marshaled the rest of the family to action. "Monji, get the kids some clothes and put them in a backpack. James, you get some more fruit from the backyard. Marbu, see if you can gather together a plastic jug of water for each person. Come on!" He barked like an army sergeant.

"There's enough daylight left for us to get to my uncle's house by dark."

Suah meant what he said, but it was a fresh round of gunfire in the distance that suddenly made them all want to hurry. Within a few minutes the family was ready to go. After the trauma on the field the previous night, nothing would have felt as good as sleeping in their comfortable beds. But leave them they must.

The road to Uncle Sundagar's house was not so far. Only a few miles, and as discouraging as it was hitting the road this time of day, every mile they put between them and Charles Taylor's men made them feel safer. As the shouting and gunshots grew more and more faint, Marbu dared to breathe a sigh of relief. God had helped them all escape, and he was eternally grateful. Otherwise they would all likely be still on the field in Paynesville or marched off down the road to face a firing squad.

Such troubling thoughts kept running through Marbu's head, and he knew he needed to put them out of his mind. He needed to focus now on what lay ahead.

Uncle Sundagar was glad to see them all safe, but not really surprised. "I half expected to see you a few days back when all the troubles started," he said as they all sat down to bowls of rice and fish.

Chapter 6

We would have come, and probably should have, but there was gunfire everywhere, so for several days we just laid low. No one ventured out." Suah told Sundagar of the nightmarish ordeal on the open field in town and of sneaking back to the house to get food and water.

"That sounds like you, Suah. Always the one to dare the odds. I think I would have stayed put on the commons."

"But we had no idea how long they were going to keep us." Suah looked indignant.

Uncle Sundagar shook his head stubbornly. "Doesn't matter, if one of you had been shot, what would you have said then?"

"We figured we were all going to be shot soon anyway!"

"So that's why you went back to get the clothes and water, right?"

At this rate Marbu could see they were going to argue all night. Instead of being grateful for the lives of these family members, Sundagar only wanted to criticize. Marbu finally stepped out of the house into the darkness. "Thank You, God," he breathed a prayer of thanksgiving as he stared up at the night sky. "You were so good to let us escape and see another day."

They stayed with Uncle Sundagar for nearly a week, but each day they could hear gunfire increasing and getting closer. Sundagar's house was quite a distance from the main road, but Marbu could see truckloads of soldiers going into Paynesville almost daily.

"I don't like the looks of this," Marbu confessed to Suah one day when he came out to watch a new parade of vehicles along the river road. "Things are heating up down there."

"Looks like it, doesn't it?" Suah squinted at the long line of slow-moving trucks. "I think we know what we've got to do, but Monji's not going to like it."

That night around the evening meal, Suah announced the next move. "We can't stay here any longer. Rebel forces could come any day. I hear they're starting to draw recruits for Taylor's army from the local towns in the area. And of course there's always the chance they could accuse us of being supportive of the Krahn tribe again. The question is Where do we go from here?" he added.

"We could go east toward Marshall. Kokou, our half brother, lives there," Marbu offered.

"That's a good idea," Suah said, nodding at his younger brother, but Monji didn't look happy at all.

"Can't we just stay here with Uncle Sundagar?" she frowned. "It'll be safe enough."

"We're leaving." Suah ignored his wife's protest. "It would be nice to hope this war will soon be over, but if Taylor should overthrow President Doe's government, things could get pretty shaky here near the coast. And then there's Prince Johnson, and at least two other revolutionary leaders marching toward the capital. No matter who's in power, there's going to be lots of fighting around here for a while, and I'm not sure which one we'd be better off with in the capital. I'm all for Marbu's idea. Let's head to Marshall. Things are sure to be a bit safer there."

The next morning they all headed out again with what they could carry. It was the saddest sight you could ever see. Everyone was carrying a pack of some kind, even the children. They carried food and a few plastic jugs for water, enough to last the few days they figured it would take them to walk to Marshall. They would have hired a car to take them the distance, but of course no one was out on the roads, with all the military action. Everyone was holed up out of sight, afraid of what was coming next.

All that day the refugees walked the road heading east. Sometimes they heard gunfire or military trucks coming along the road, and then everybody would quickly disappear into the jungle. The children fussed and Monji fretted, but they passed the day without mishap, stopping to rest in the shade during the hottest part of the day. By late afternoon the children were getting tired, so everybody helped carry them. The men wanted to get as far as they could that first day while their energy was at its highest. "The farther we go, the quicker we'll get there," Suah said confidently, "and that's what's important now."

They traveled a greater distance that first day than Marbu would have thought possible. As the afternoon hours waned, a refreshing breeze blew up from the ocean to the south, which seemed to help some. The little band of refugees walked until the shadows from the setting sun stretched their long fingers across the road. As twilight descended upon them, the road ahead became harder and harder to see. Suah finally ordered them to stop for the night, and they laid out their sleeping mats in a small clearing.

"We can't afford to light a fire," Suah said. "We never know who might be coming along the road this time of night." They ate a quick meal, and the rice and cold sweet potatoes tasted good after the many miles they had walked. The moon and stars came out and added a sprinkling of light to the night sky. Marbu wondered how many bands of refugees had camped out under a starlit sky in all the wars through all the ages of the world. He guessed there must have been thousands and millions.

But that was where the nostalgia of camping on the road ended. Marbu was worried that the family would fare poorly with malaria-infested mosquitoes on the prowl. Without a smoky fire, mosquitoes were always more of a problem, and tonight would be no different.

Please, Lord, protect us from our worst enemy, Marbu begged God. How many people in Liberia suffered every night from the little blood-sucking insects? Then again, how many armies traipsing up and down the coast had been brought to a halt by the sickness these mosquitoes carried?

The evening was warm and muggy as they all stretched out for the night, but memories of standing in the hot sun for two days at the checkpoint helped keep the little band thankful. All except Monji. She fussed and grumbled about the inconveniences of the open road, but one hard look from Suah made her hold her tongue.

Marbu lay on his back staring up at the stars. He found it hard to believe that Monji could be so ungrateful when she should have been praising God for their miraculous escape in Paynesville. But then he realized her problem was that she didn't trust God as she should. Instead of faulting her for her lack of faith and the complaining spirit that seemed to plague her every step, he needed to remind her of God's goodness.

Like her husband, Monji was not really a Christian. She had been sprinkled as a baby by the Catholic Church, but that was about the extent of her religious experience. In the small band of refugees, Marbu was the only Seventh-day Adventist.

"I think we should thank God for His protection," Marbu finally said. "I've been thinking about the checkpoint and how long we had to wait for them to clear us with our identity papers. At first none of us wanted to be interrogated for fear of what was coming. And then as the time wore on and we all got so hot and thirsty, I think everyone wanted to get on with it. It's like we wanted it one way, and then we wanted it the other. We didn't really know what we wanted. We just wanted relief.

"And although some of us complained, God in His wisdom didn't let our family through that checkpoint in a hurry. Now I think I know why. When we finally did get to go through, the commandos were tired and worn out. Almost as much as us, maybe, which is why they probably let us leave after asking only a few questions."

"You think so?" Suah turned on his mat toward Marbu.

"I do," Marbu nodded in the darkness. "Think about it. The first day and a half they yanked people from the line right and left to be led away and shot. We know for a fact some were not from the Krahn tribe." Marbu let his words sink in. "We could have died back in Paynesville, Suah, but God in His goodness has seen fit to give us another day of life."

Marbu closed his eyes and began to pray out loud for the benefit of the family. "Lord, we are so grateful for Your protection. We are complainers like the children of Israel in the wilderness so long ago, but we are confident You are watching over us. In the face of death You have delivered us, and still we are ungrateful it seems. Forgive us, Lord. May we be more thankful tomorrow, and may You see us safely to our destination, where we can rest at last."

Suah didn't say a word, and no one else did either, but Marbu was sure now it wasn't because they were ungrateful. His words had given them all food for thought. It seemed to be a solemn moment for them all, and the reality of the past week was finally beginning to settle in. That, and they were all so very tired. They had escaped from the clutches of certain death, and now their tired bodies needed rest. Soon everyone was fast asleep and resting well in spite of the hard ground. But then, that shouldn't have been a surprise. After all, they were under the watchful care of guardian angels.

But their troubles weren't over. Actually, they were just beginning. If Marbu could have pulled back a curtain to see what was coming in the next few days, he might have found his faith faltering.

Chapter 7

The night passed quickly, and when Marbu awakened, he hardly remembered even falling asleep. But he felt rested, and he thanked his heavenly Father for this added blessing. And then suddenly the morning road was being flooded with refugees from Monrovia and other outlying villages along the coast. Marbu knew very few of them, but now and then he spotted someone he recognized. Marbu was eating a quick breakfast of cold manioc when he spotted Otis, an old friend from his childhood, passing by on the road.

"Otis!" Marbu called out to the young man in the crowd of straggling refugees. "Stop and have a little something to eat!" Otis looked tired and rumpled, a sure sign he had slept somewhere on the ground too, but he smiled now at the sight of Marbu. Monji handed the young man some manioc on a banana leaf as the young men got reacquainted.

Otis and Marbu had grown up together in the same town. They had even attended the same school at one time. Like Marbu, Otis wasn't married, and he wasn't with his family at the time of the raid, so this made his flight from Paynesville somewhat easier. He too had escaped the fate of many who had been rooted out by Charles Taylor's men, though he worried about his mother and father and two sisters.

With breakfast over, the family got on the road again. As they headed east, Marbu and Otis talked of old memories. They reiminisced about fishing in the creeks and playing African football and snaring gophers, or grass cutters as everyone called them, to sell at the market.

Those carefree days seemed so long ago now. There was so much more to deal with in life than childhood games. So much had changed with the nightmare of civil war all around them. And yet a common thread was still there between the two of them, regardless of the circumstances. Both were refugees on the road, exiled from home with little food and no shelter, but they did have their freedom.

Marbu and Otis talked of school and family and even girls. But eventually their conversation fell to talk of the war now raging all around them. "I was so scared when I heard the guns going off," Otis said with a look of anger and fear on his face. "What is wrong with our people! Must we always fight like animals? It makes me sick, I tell you, and I hate it!" He glared at the early-morning sun. "But what's the use of talking about it! We'll never change!"

Marbu knew his friend was right. Seeing a civil war waged in your backyard by revolutionaries was a hard thing. It seemed so pointless! So unfair! This was not their war! It belonged to government officials. It belonged to Charles Taylor and the other revolutionary leaders running raids up and down the coast of Liberia. Unfortunately, good people got caught in the middle of it all. Decent, ordinary people who wanted nothing more than to earn a good living, provide for their families, and send their children to school.

Just thinking about it made Marbu glad he was a Christian. Being a Christian didn't really change things as far as the war was concerned, but being a Seventh-day Adventist Christian did. It helped him deal with all the questions that had been running through his head during the past few weeks. Being a Seventh-day Adventist gave him perspective when it came to tragedies such as war. He understood that the goal of Satan's government was to destroy people and defame God's character. The devil had been at war with God since the early days in heaven when the great controversy between good and evil began. Satan hates God and all things good. The more pain and sadness he can inflict on humanity, the more satisfied he feels. This philosophy and understanding of the Bible helped Marbu more than anything in dealing with all the upheaval around him.

But Marbu couldn't tell Otis all this. His friend wouldn't understand much of it. Marbu could tell him of the peace that God offers to those who ask for it, and that's where he knew it all had to start.

"I'm like you," Marbu said sadly. "I can see that this war makes no sense, and I have to wonder when it will all end. But, hey! That's a worry for tomorrow. Today we're alive! God preserved us from death, and right now we can be grateful for it!" Marbu pointed at the sky. "God will take care of us. He's promised it in the Bible. If we just call upon Him, He will answer. The Bible says, 'In my distress I cried to the Lord, and He heard me'" (Ps. 120:1). Marbu was surprised at how easily he could recite the verses of Scripture as they popped into his head. It was as if God had put them there.

"You make it sound so easy." Otis's eyes softened a bit at the mention of God. "I wish God would deliver me out this distress! I wish He would deliver us all out of this distress."

"He can!" Marbu didn't miss a beat. "Just believe in the Lord Jesus Christ and you shall be saved."

"Saved? Saved from what?" Otis looked confused. "There's this war going on right now, and that's all I care about." He scowled again.

"Saved now, saved later; it's all part of the same thing." Marbu glanced at Otis again. "If God has you like this"—Marbu put his hands together—"then it's all taken care of. It doesn't matter what happens to us when or where or how. God has us in the palm of His hand, and when you stop and think about it, that's all that really matters."

Otis stopped arguing. "I never thought about it like that before. I'm not much of a Christian, I guess. Most of my family are Catholics, and they still worship spirits. None of us have been to church in years. I wish I could have your kind of faith."

"You can." Marbu stopped in the middle of the road for a moment and looked at Otis. "You can have it right here, now. All you have to do is claim that promise, and God has you covered." Marbu put his hand on Otis's shoulder, and they started walking again. "Bad things happen to good people, Otis, but God will make sure it all turns out good in the end. You can count on it. As sure as the sun rises and sets each day, God loves you and wants what is best for you."

Marbu suddenly realized what was happening. A friend on a road teeming with refugees desperately needed hope, and God was using Marbu to give it to him. And where was Marbu getting all these simple lines of Christian logic? The words just came to him as they walked along. It was like a mini Bible study without his ever having planned it out. Marbu remembered a Bible verse somewhere that said God would give a person the right words to say when he or she needed to share God's love with others. Jesus had said it Himself, hadn't He? The idea was truly amazing, and Marbu knew beyond a shadow of a doubt that this was exactly what was happening to him right now.

As Marbu walked that Liberian road, his mind focused on the most basic beliefs of his young life. Maybe some things were not exactly what they appeared to be. Maybe for Marbu there was more to this senseless war than just escaping death. Maybe it was about taking the opportunity to introduce people to the Lord of the ages, a God who could deliver people out of their distresses. And maybe this was the only way some people in Liberia would ever be able to encounter the love of Jesus.

There on the road of refugees plodding eastward in the hot morning sun, Marbu had an epiphany that some people take a lifetime to find. God's love for His wayward children was real, even for those who weren't especially looking for Him. God sometimes allowed bad things to happen so that good people would discern His saving grace. God was walking with those who needed Him most, even during times of war and bloodshed.

Such concepts might have seemed incomprehensible to Marbu before, but here they were being demonstrated in a most remarkable way, and Otis was living proof of it. Otis needed to know about the infinitely compassionate God who sees and knows all things, and Marbu could introduce him to the Creator. Right here. Right now. No fancy altar call. No big evangelistic scheme. Just God and Marbu and Otis. It was a moment Marbu planned to remember for the rest of his life.

They had been on the road for two days now, and food was running out. They had only a little bit of rice left and some manioc. Marbu and Otis managed to find a few papayas on a jungle trail off the road, but there was little else. Others had stripped the fruit before them.

About dark they reached the town of Pipeline. The last shades of day were fading as they walked up the little dirt road into town. Trying to remain as inconspicuous as possible, they finally stopped under some coconut palms to rest and make plans for the night. They were exhausted from walking all day in the hot sun. They had found little to eat, and the idea of spending another night on the hard, bug-infested ground was a discouraging thought. And now what would they find to eat this time of night? Where would they find a safe place to sleep? They had little money with them. Would anybody care that they were refugees who needed help? Could they even trust these townspeople?

Chapter 8

As the shadows of dusk deepened, a jeep suddenly rounded the corner and roared down the street. There was no time to run, no time to hide. Marbu's heart raced as the jeep slowed to a crawl. Was it some of General Taylor's commandos coming to round the refugees up again? Had the long, tiring journey from Paynesville been all for nothing? To Marbu's surprise, a soldier leaned out of the jeep and shouted, "You folks had better find cover! There's going to be gunfire pretty quick here!"

"Not again!" Monji scowled, but Marbu was thankful for the tip.

"Come on, everybody! We've got to get going!" Suah urged, getting everyone to their feet. "We don't need any more of a warning than that!"

Marbu was a bit mystified. Who were these friendly soldiers, and why had they bothered to warn the refugees of the coming danger? Were they angels in disguise? Just the day before Marbu and the other refugees had feared for their lives while facing such soldiers, but now these revolutionaries were offering friendly advice? Whether they were Taylor's men or angels, Marbu didn't stop to ponder the situation. The advice had been timely, and that was all they needed to get out of harm's way.

But where should they go? They knew no one in town, and the idea of moving on down the road this time of night was disheartening, if not downright dangerous. Marbu and his brothers were afraid to ask anyone for help, but what choice did they have.

"I say we trust God to help us," Marbu finally said. "He didn't bring us this far to leave us stranded."

"OK, but how does that help us?" Suah stared at Marbu.

Marbu pointed at the first house up the road. "I'm going to knock on that door over there and ask the people if we can stay with them for the night. What have we got to lose?"

"They can turn us down," Suah said skeptically.

"Then we ask at the next place," Marbu stated matter-of-factly. He turned and started up the street, ignoring his brother's negativity. Within seconds he was knocking on the door of a complete stranger, and wonder of wonders, the old folks inside were kind and gracious. Amazingly, the

Mensahs welcomed Marbu's family in and allowed them to sleep on the floor in one of the rooms. They even brought out some rice they had cooked for their own family and shared it with the refugees.

"God bless you," Marbu said with tears in his eyes. He had not expected God to give them such blessings so soon—it was clear his family was also deeply moved by this kind act. Once again, God had provided for them in a strange town by giving them a place that was hospitable. Who knew how many other homes in town would have been as giving.

And it was a good thing they found shelter. All that night rockets blazed in the night sky, exploding overhead and raining shrapnel down on the rooftops.

Marbu began to wonder what was so strategic about this small town that the enemy had chosen it for a battlefield. Would they come knocking on doors the next morning? *Please, Lord,* he found himself praying again, *keep us safe under Your care. You've done that so many times already in the past couple weeks. Keep my faith in You strong, Lord. I want to trust in You completely, so give me the courage now to do that. And may I be a witness to my own family.*

He finally dozed, but somewhere in the night he wakened again to the boom and roar of the incessant rockets. Were the rocket launches getting more frequent? Was the battle heating up? He closed his eyes to shut out the flashes of light, but the explosions sometimes were so bright it seemed as if morning had come.

"*He who dwells in the secret place of the Most High shall abide under the shadow of the Almighty.*" Marbu began praying again, reciting a chapter of Scripture he had memorized when he was much younger. "*I will say of the Lord, 'He is my refuge and my fortress, my God, in Him I will trust.'*" The exploding mortars above the rooftops threatened to drown out his thoughts. "*Surely He shall deliver you from the snare of the fowler, and from the perilous pestilence. He shall cover you with His feathers, and under His wings you shall take refuge; His truth shall be your shield and buckler. You shall not be afraid of the terror by night, nor of the arrow that flies*" (Ps. 91:1-5). Somewhere in that part of the verse Marbu faded off to sleep once again.

But he was up again early the next morning. The rockets were finally silent, and Marbu guessed the soldiers had grown tired of their war games. Dawn had not yet streaked the eastern sky, but he was anxious for his family to be on their way. By daylight everyone was ready to get a good start before the heat of the day set in. The Mensah family gave them some rice and manioc wrapped in banana leaves for the journey, and then off they went.

As they turned down one street, friendly commandos at the town entrance sent Marbu and his family up the road to Kakata. "It's a detour route," they said, "but the way is clear."

As usual there was no means of transport, and the refugees had to walk. They made pretty good time during the morning hours, but by afternoon the sun beat down on them mercilessly. July was usually a rather wet month, but for some reason this season was particularly dry, and the dusty roads made life miserable for the travelers. The family stopped to rest during the hottest part of the day. When big trucks came by, everyone scrambled off into the elephant grass. They could hide there from the soldiers who might do them harm, but they could not escape the dust. Marbu tried to close his eyes and hold a cloth over his mouth to keep out the choking clouds of dust, but it did him very little good. And then Suah's two youngest children got tired and had to be carried.

About midafternoon they all reached a fork in the road where a sign pointed east to Marshall. After a brief stop for water, they headed in that direction. Their spirits were high as they continued down the road. About a mile later the road turned and entered the river bottom where the jungle growth was quite thick. Here and there along the road were pathways that led into the luxuriant foliage. Marbu wondered what kinds of wild beasts hid themselves there during the heat of the day.

Might there be lions? Likely not, since all the big game along this part of the coast had long since been killed off by poachers. The only ones alive now were on game reserves farther north. There were probably a few big pythons, though, and lots of green and black mambas. Snakes always made Marbu shiver. It wasn't that he hadn't seen enough of them; he had chased them as a boy. It was more because this place was so remote. If anyone got bitten out here by a mamba, there would be no chance of getting any kind of medical help in time.

"Protect us, Lord," Marbu found himself praying once again. "We are asking You to do for us what we cannot do for ourselves."

He had no sooner finished his prayer when a commando suddenly came streaking out from a jungle pathway, shouting, "There's an ambush ahead!" and then raced west down the road they had just traveled. There was no time to guess what exactly the commando meant or where the danger actually lay, but everyone acted instinctively as they had done many times before on this trip. Immediately they melted into the jungle and waited to see what would happen. For over an hour they laid low. It was only when they heard trucks driving away to the east that they finally emerged from the jungle. However, they now thought it better to return west by way of the road they had come.

Returning to the sign they had passed more than an hour before, they hurried up the other fork of the dusty road to Waka, another small town on their route. As they plodded along, Marbu bowed his head to thank his heavenly Father. *You are so good, Lord, and I thank You for sending us the warning on the trail.* Marbu had no idea what they had been facing on the jungle road, but he was sure it had once again been a narrow escape.

Marbu's thoughts turned to his family and their seeming disregard for the obvious reasons they were still alive. Could they not see it? God had preserved them, and though many in the group had a Christian background, not one of them had given the Lord credit except Otis. God had provided narrow escapes from death for them all, and still they showed no gratefulness to God. If they understood the irony of it all, they were not admitting it, and that was just plain wrong! Jesus was their help and strength, and they needed to honor and thank Him for it. How many times must God reveal Himself before they would recognize the heavenly protection and power surrounding them?

Chapter 9

Marbu glanced around him at the group and suddenly stopped in the middle of the road. He had to say something in God's favor. It was the right thing to do! It was the only thing to do! "God is the reason we are all still alive," Marbu said adamantly. "You all know it's true. He saved us from death at the checkpoint in Paynesville. He sent soldiers last night to give us directions about where we should go. He gave us a place to stay in the little town of Pipeline, and He protected us from rocket fire there. He preserved us just now from an ambush. I'm not positive, but that might have been an angel who warned us to hide. God has kept us by the power of His guardian angels these many times, and we have Him to thank for it."

"You're right," Suah admitted, bowing his head. "We must be grateful." The group was unusually quiet as they started on their way again. They couldn't deny the truth of Marbu's inspiring words. It was true, and it was becoming increasingly clear that God was guiding and protecting them on their journey. He alone was behind what appeared to be a string of miracles on their behalf.

Just before dark they reached the little town of Waka, and again God provided a place for them to stay with kind strangers they had never met. George Dwede and his family warmly invited them to stay the night. To make room for the strangers the five children in the family had to crowd into the back room of the house with their parents, generously giving up their sleeping mats.

"This is very kind of you!" Marbu told the young family. "We thank you for your goodness, and we pray that God will bless your home for it."

They all rested well that night, but the next morning when Marbu was out on a short walk, he suddenly stumbled upon a commando patrolling the streets. There was no chance to avoid the soldier—Marbu hadn't seen him in time to make a detour.

"Where are you from?" the commando asked when he saw the look of fear in Marbu's eyes.

Marbu didn't recognize the uniform, and his heart nearly stopped. Was this soldier one of Charles Taylor's men? "I'm up from Paynesville with my family," Marbu stammered, but he said nothing more. Better to let this commando think he was visiting family than to tell him he was a refugee. But he should have known better than to think he could fool the revolutionary.

"You'd better clear out of Waka while you can," the commando said as he checked the ammunition clip on his M-16. "Prince Johnson is headed this way. He'll be taking the town and anyone that's left in it."

"When?" Marbu stared at the soldier in amazement.

"By noon, we expect."

"Are you with Charles Taylor?" Marbu dared to ask.

"Nope! I'm with Prince Johnson." The commando said nothing more as he put his rifle strap over his shoulder and continued on his rounds.

Marbu hurried home and burst in on the family eating a breakfast of fou-fou and rice. "We've got to leave now!" he shouted

Suah looked up in surprise. "Why, what's happened?"

"Prince Johnson is on his way with his guerrillas. A commando told me we've got only a few hours." Marbu began gathering up his few things and pushing them into his backpack.

"Was he militant?"

"No, actually he was quite nice." Marbu grabbed up a few bananas and shoved them into his pack. "The commando offered the information without me asking for it, as if he didn't want any of us to get hurt."

Their host, Mr. Dwede, stood up and glanced out the window. "What color of uniform was the commando wearing?"

"The usual. Gray-green with slashes of tan." Marbu thought a moment, "And he was wearing a black beret."

"That's one of Johnson's men all right. I know some of the officers in his brigade. I heard they might come this way, and I guess they've finally made it."

"Where do you think we should go?" Suah saw his wife's crestfallen face.

"I don't know. I hadn't thought that far ahead," Marbu admitted. "Usually you're the one who makes those kinds of decisions."

"I've been thinking," said James, Marbu's younger brother. He was usually the quiet one, but now he ventured an opinion. "It seems we'll wear Monji and the kids out if we keep running. If these soldiers of Johnson seem nice enough, maybe Suah and his family would actually be safer here than out on the road."

Monji's eyes lit up for the first time in days. It looked as if a ton of bricks had rolled off her back. Suah glanced at his brothers, and then at his wife again. "Maybe you're right," he finally said.

"Well, I'm leaving," Marbu announced. "I don't really know who we can trust anymore. I say we go north away from the fighting. Moving on toward Kakata, as we were advised, is better any day than being a sitting duck here. It's our only hope if we want to make it out of this thing alive." He glanced at Otis. "Are you coming with me?"

"You bet I am!" Otis nodded. "I wouldn't let you go without me." He, too, began gathering up his things.

"How about you, James?"

"Sure, I'll go. I've got nothing to wait around here for."

And so it was the boys headed north on foot, traveling again on the road to Kakata. Other refugees on the road joined them until there were 11 in the group. One of the men, Gartee, had four children and his wife with him.

They had plenty of time to talk as they walked. They shared family news and general information about where they were from, what the menfolk did for a living, and of course the latest about what was happening in the recent civil war. But as always, Marbu eventually worked the conversation around to things of God, and he finally asked Gartee if he was a Christian.

"Not much of one," Gartee said good-naturedly, "but I guess all the trouble lately has brought me a little bit more to my senses. I suppose everyone should think about God some, especially with the war going on."

"We've all suffered much hardship during the last few days," Marbu agreed, "so it's natural that we might think more about God." His heart went out to Gartee, and he suddenly felt the need to say something that would make a difference in the man's life. "In spite of all the destruction and violence around us, God is still our only hope," Marbu stated.

"It's true," Gartee nodded, "but I can't help asking myself where God is at a time like this, with all the horrors of war going on."

"Have you seen people being executed as we have?"

"I'll say I have. Right now I'm trying to put it all out of my mind, but I'm not having much luck of it. Like you say, these are hard times. It is hard not to let things get you down."

"Well, I've got good news," Marbu replied. "Did you know that Jesus is coming again very soon to take us all to heaven with Him? When He comes, He'll give us a new life with Him that will never again be ruined by pain or suffering or death. The Bible is very plain about such things."

"Really?" Gartee scratched his chin. "Well, no one preaches that sort of thing in the churches I've been to."

"You're right, and that's too bad." Marbu picked a stem of grass along the roadway and began chewing on it. "But the important thing to remember is that today and every day God is offering you and me eternal life. Do you believe that?"

"I guess I do. I can't argue with a good thing, can I?"

"Good; then it's settled. Very soon here you will probably go your way and I mine, but we shall see each other again in the earth made new! What do you say?"

"I say amen to that, brother!"

It was a lighthearted sort of conversation for the terrible times they were living in, but Marbu felt it was the best thing they could have talked about under the circumstances.

Marbu wanted to ask Gartee what he was doing with so many children out on the road, but the man seemed so carefree after their conversation about God that Marbu didn't have the heart to ask him. And besides, Suah himself had been on the road for several days with his family. *I guess he must feel it's better to stick together than get split up*, Marbu thought.

Chapter 10

The refugees kept to the dusty back roads, but the group made pretty good time. It was a country road, so they had no mishaps that first day. When they came to a coconut plantation, they cut open a dozen coconuts with the machete Otis was carrying and drank the cool milk.

By nightfall they were in the middle of nowhere, but they stopped to get some sleep. "I'm glad Suah kept his family in Waka," James said tiredly as they stretched out on the ground to sleep once again. "I don't think I could have taken another night listening to Monji fuss. I think that woman would almost rather die than be inconvenienced."

Somewhere on the night wind they could hear jungle drums beating, and everybody knew what that meant. Judging by the tone and rhythm of the beat, someone in a village nearby had died recently. Marbu stared up at the night sky and wondered who it might be. Was it an old man who had lived a long and eventful life? Was it a child, still in the habit of riding on his mother's back to the fields or the market? Was it a young man killed in the skirmishes of the civil war?

Marbu closed his eyes as he thought about the African culture in which he had been born and raised. Fortunately, he was a Christian, or he would have lived in fear, as so many of his family did concerning the death of a family member. The legends and myths of West African culture taught that an African who dies gets into a boat and crosses over the great lake of the spirit world to get to the shores of eternity on the other side. An African who has been kind to the dead while they were living will be greeted by the spirits with smiles of acceptance. However, an African who has snubbed the spirits in life will not be allowed to land their boat, and will be pushed back out by the spirits, to drift in punishment for their sins of neglect.

In Marbu's world this fear of death permeated every aspect of village life. The cultural celebrations held in the villages of Liberia to honor the spirits of the dead were just one example. Strange things happened at these dances when the shadows of night had fallen on the streets. Marbu was glad to be free of their fearful grip. He was glad to know the truth about God and what happens when you die.

At these dances huge bonfires blazed in the city streets while painted bodies pranced in weird chaotic circles. Drugged with alcohol and stupefying drugs such as the kola nut, men would dance themselves to a frenzy until it was clear their bodies were possessed by demons of the darkness. Their eyes would glaze over as their bodies grew stiff. In these rituals many would pull knives from their belts and slash themselves viciously until the blood flowed freely. Some would even plunge the knives into their abdomen, allowing their organs to protrude from the gaping wounds.

Marbu had heard of cases in which the wounded man would pull out his intestines, play with them in his hands as if they were a string of sausage, and then push them back inside. This would of course send the man into a state of shock, from which he would eventually collapse in the dust of the street.

However, sometimes when the magic was strong and the power of the witch man's voodoo had been purchased at a price, demonic healings took place. In these cases the injured man would reach into a pouch at his side, pull out a mysterious, sticky yellow paste given him by the witch doctor, and rub it on the wound. The cut would heal instantly with the help of unseen forces.

The popular Christian churches of Liberia did not take part in these rituals, but many did not forbid them, either. The Catholic Church had been present in this part of Africa for hundreds of years, but they seemed to care little if the locals practiced their cultural rites. As long as the common folks came to holy Mass once in a while, partook of the Eucharist, and bought intercessory candles, the priests tolerated the village practices of pagan animism.

One of the most popular celebrations in the village life of West Africa was the dance of the mask festival. This was a time for people to come together and observe the traditions of their past—a time for eating pig and rats and snake meat—a time for young men of the tribe to strut their passage into manhood.

But more than anything else it was a feast day to celebrate the villagers' fascination with the macabre of death, a dance to honor the spirits of those long departed. At the main ceremony of the feast, designated men danced in a slow arching circle in the village square. Each dancer held a carved wooden mask to his face and danced to the pulsating thud of dull rhythmic drums used for such occasions. At the center of the dancers was a large wooden mask propped upright in the village square. The mask had slits for eyes, long flowing hair made from frayed straw and bark, and strange painted markings that represented the tribe from which it came.

The dancers drank strong potions until their minds were clouded in a drunken state. As the night deepened and the ceremony progressed toward its crescendo, the speed of the drums increased, and the dancers jumped and twitched as if their bodies were on fire. Slowly and mysteriously the large wooden mask at the center of the crowd would then begin to move. Rising up from the ground, it would sway and dance to the rhythm of the drums, making the villagers "ooh" and "aah" in wonder.

The lingering thoughts of village dancers and masks and devil worship made Marbu shiver. As a Christian he stayed away from feasts that honored the dancing mask. The power of Satan was in these places. His presence was as real as the heavy bonfire smoke drifting through the village streets and alleys. It seemed that these dark traditions of superstition and ignorance held sway in every village, and Marbu wondered if his family would ever be able to escape them.

But there were other forces equally as powerful in the life of an African. The strength of tribalism could be oppressive, and it was everywhere. A man's religion might hold him in its superstitious grip, but the loyalties to one's tribe were even more compelling. And, of course, there was always the desire for wealth. Most Africans in Liberia were considered poor, but the goal of many was to become fabulously rich and to do this by any means possible. A few fortunate ones had done it through sports, and many more by selling drugs on the black market. Government takeovers were the latest road some were making at fame and fortune.

The 1960s saw a chain of historical events that changed the face of West Africa. In many countries along the coast the old generation had thrown off the yoke of European colonialism and liberated themselves in the name of democracy. But as was often the case, the new leadership eventually gained absolute power, and then they ruled with an iron fist by forming a dictatorship. Civil wars seemd to break out in retaliation every few years, but the government would begin a war of ruthless genocide.

The cycle was a vicious one with no permanent solution in sight. Every new generation it seemed must suffer until they, in turn, overthrew the regimes of the old order. The wheels of progress were turned by politics, and politics was fueled by money and tribal racism. Samuel Doe's dictatorship had become part of this process, but so had General Charles

Taylor and the other three revolutionaries trying to gain control of the Liberian government.

The hard ground was lumpy, and Marbu tried to find a comfortable position in which to sleep, but eventually he just lay flat on his back and used his backpack as a pillow. His eyes followed the star-spangled Milky Way as it stretched across the heavens of the night sky. "Lord, I want to thank You for being in control of this world," he prayed. "Dictators rise and fall, governments come and go, but You will always be up there among the stars, directing the universe from Your throne. It makes me feel safe, Lord." And with that Marbu finally slept.

The next morning the band of refugees was off again. Not wanting to waste the little bit of water they had with them to wash their faces, they set out looking dusty and grimy.

By midmorning Marbu and his group came to a rubber plantation and a road sign that said "15-gate." Up ahead a short distance Marbu saw people standing near a checkpoint of some sort.

"You guys stay here," Marbu told Otis and his brother. "I'm going to go see if it's safe enough for us to pass by this way, or if we should go back the way we came." He circled around through a patch of jungle along the road to get a better view of the checkpoint, when he suddenly stumbled upon a man's body in the pathway. Was the man dead? It certainly looked like it.

Chapter 11

M arbu stared in horror at the man's lifeless form. He had begun to put the frightening days of Paynesville behind him, and now this! A dead body here was the last thing he had expected to find. The body was covered with blood and quite lifeless. Marbu wasn't sure, but he guessed the man had been dead only a short while. There weren't any flies around yet, but even so there was the distinct smell of death in the air.

And then suddenly Marbu recognized the man. It was Gartee, the man they had been traveling with on the road from Waka. Only 20 minutes before, Gartee had been with them as they approached the checkpoint. Now he was dead. Marbu couldn't move as he stared at the poor man. *Life is too short*, he thought. Just that afternoon the two of them had shared a wonderful conversation about the fate of everyone who makes their choice for God and eternity. Marbu was so glad now that he had dared to share his testimony with Gartee, and that the man had made a commitment for Jesus. It was the last real chance Gartee had had to prepare himself for eternal life.

Marbu felt himself growing queasy at the sight of all that blood. Judging by the cuts on Gartee, he had been killed with a machete. Marbu hadn't heard any screams or anyone calling for help. How had the killer managed to do such a deed without the crowd of refugees hearing? The body wasn't that far from the group gathered together out on the road.

And then suddenly an eerie chill ran down Marbu's spine as it occurred to him that he was probably in danger too. Here he was standing in this remote spot off the road, a refugee far from home with nothing to defend himself. Those who killed Gartee might come back to kill him. Panic gripped Marbu, and he wanted to run far away from this horrible place! He turned and hurried back to where James and Otis were waiting and told them the horrible news.

"He was just here a few minutes ago!" Otis groaned. "I've got a very bad feeling about this place."

Quickly the men sneaked through the jungle on an escape route past the checkpoint. They walked for more than an hour, until they reached the edge of the forest on the outskirts of Kakata. And what a sight met their eyes! The place was strewn with dead bodies everywhere! Guerrilla commandos walked among the dead, stripping them of any valuables they could find.

Hundreds of villagers were everywhere, many of them refugees, and some no doubt citizens from the town of Kakata. Many stood in lines as they had back at the checkpoints in Paynesville. Others were on their knees in the dirt, cowering in fear at the barrels of AK-47s pointed in their faces. Soldiers were confiscating whatever money or personal belongings the people had.

Suddenly the staccato of machine gunfire sprayed the leaves of the jungle behind Marbu, and he instinctively dropped to the ground. James and Otis fell to the ground too, and then they were surrounded by several commandos out on patrol.

"So! You thought you'd avoid the checkpoint!" one of the soldiers sneered. Marbu and the others tried to get to their feet, but one of the commandos hit Otis across the back of the neck with the butt of his rifle! Otis staggered but managed to stay on his feet.

The commandos demanded anything of value Marbu and the others might have on them. Marbu had managed to keep his watch hidden until now. James had some money sewed in a cloth belt hidden under his shirt around his waist, but he dared not conceal it any longer. The extra clothes Marbu and James had with them were confiscated too. Otis had nothing to give, so they beat him senseless until he was bloodied and nearly unconscious.

Marbu was stunned at this turn of events! How had they let themselves walk into this trap! Why hadn't he and the others kept to the small villages instead of venturing near towns such as Kakata where they should have known there would be enemy soldiers! It made Marbu sick to think that here they were again, captives at the hands of cruel mercenaries, being exploited and robbed of everything they owned, including their dignity.

The commandos were more of Charles Taylor's men, known for their violence and crude methods of getting what they wanted. Within the hour they had rounded up everyone and began marching them on the road east out of Kakata. Where were they being taken? Marbu had no idea. He had never been in this part of the country before.

He stared up at the bright sky as if he were in a trance. He was walking along the road with family and friends in a crowd of refugees, and yet he felt very much alone. It was a strange feeling. Where was God now? The Lord had delivered Marbu so many times already on this trip, but those marvels of God's goodness were far from Marbu's mind now. How easily he could forget, it seemed.

All that pressed to the front of his mind at this moment were feelings of despair. Would he and the others have to suffer more hardships? Without doubt. Would they have to wait again to be interrogated about their identity? Probably. Would they be beaten and abused? Already Otis had been thrashed within an inch of his life, it seemed. The huge welt on his head now oozed dangerously, and he had cuts and bruises that defied treatment on the open road. Worse yet, would they all be taken to some remote place and shot?

For the first time since the war had started, Marbu began to seriously doubt God. *Where was He? Why was He allowing this endless round of intimidation and abuse by Taylor's commandos? Why was He permitting such treatment that seemed to violate all the laws of human decency?* The refugees had been on the road for days now without proper food or water or shelter. And they were being treated like animals by people who themselves were acting more like beasts than men!

Otis was nearly dead from a beating, and Gartee had been murdered. Marbu didn't know where Gartee's wife and children were, if they were alive at all. Maybe Gartee had been a member of the Krahn tribe. Maybe not. Marbu had never asked him that fateful question. Maybe he had just been another unfortunate victim of the senseless, bloodthirsty commando raids up and down the coast of Liberia!

That night Marbu, Otis, and James stayed in small mud-wattle huts along the road. Dozens of refugees crowded into the little makeshift shacks. The huts were empty, no doubt deserted by villagers who had fled when they heard General Taylor's troops were coming.

Otis moaned much of the night because of the wounds on his chest and head. Marbu tried to help ease his friend's pain, but what could he do? He had no medicine and no bandages. He wanted to cry out in the darkness to God, but his doubting heart had become a heavy stone! Instead he brooded at how unfortunate their circumstances were and what a horrific tragedy this latest turn of events had become!

After several sleepless hours in the cramped huts, Marbu could take the feelings of desperation no longer! *"Please, God!"* he cried out from the depths of his soul. *"I know You haven't brought us this far to let us die!*

Save us from these terrible men, Lord! If You only will, I know You can! The pitiful heart cry was small comfort to his pain-racked body now starved and thirsty from all he had been through.

The next day's march again took them down the road mile after mile without food or water. Finally they arrived at a place called Todee's Junction. By now everyone was dehydrated, their faces cracked and dry, and their eyes bloodshot from the dusty roads.

Otis was suffering more intensely now, and Marbu and James had to help him along much of the way. "I hate to say this, boys," James whispered, "but I think we'd better split up from now on. If we don't huddle together as a family, they can't play us against each other. We can't let them get us to that point. You know what I mean!" he said as he saw the look of fear in Otis's eyes. "We'll watch out for each other, but we've got to stay separate! They may get really mean if they think we're family!"

And then the long lines of waiting began again as the commandos interrogated each refugee at the next checkpoint. Army jeeps raced along the road into town, and soldiers patrolled the open fields. Guards stood along the forest's edge to prevent anyone from escaping into the jungle.

Chapter 12

While standing in line at the checkpoint, Marbu noticed a commando in camouflaged fatigues sitting by the gate staring at him. Every time Marbu chanced to glance that way the soldier was watching him. Like others standing around him, Marbu tried to ignore the commando, hoping the soldier might be looking at someone else; but the mercenary continued to stare him down. Marbu could tell the commando was beginning to get angry, but he didn't know what to do about it.

And then suddenly the soldier called out to Marbu in an unmistakable voice that sent a chill down Marbu's spine. "Hey! You! Get over here when I call you, worthless dog! Don't make me wait another second, or I'll cut you down where you stand!" he sneered.

"Me?" Marbu tried to act as if he had no idea what the commando was talking about, but the commando didn't fall for it. Others around Marbu refused to look in his direction, fearing they might get drawn into the confrontation too.

"Don't ignore me!" the commando shouted at Marbu, and jumped to his feet. "You know very well I'm talking to you!"

Marbu froze. His heart was hammering away in his chest as if it were a woodpecker, and his mind buzzed in a panic! What would happen next? Would the soldier kill him? Marbu glanced at his brother, but James could only stand by helplessly. There seemed to be nothing he could do to help Marbu.

Please, Lord, save me! Marbu's heart screamed out in terror. *I don't want to die! I want to live!* There was no time to kneel in the road to ask for God's protection. There was no time to bow his head in prayer or lift his eyes to heaven, but instinctively he called out to God, a habit borne from years of praying to his heavenly Father during good times and bad.

By now Marbu was shaking so badly he was afraid the soldier would see it, and that was the last thing he wanted. If the commando thought Marbu was afraid, he would probably be even more cruel.

"You're one of them, aren't you?" the soldier shouted. "You look just like a Krahn!"

"No!" Marbu stared wide-eyed at the machete hanging from the commando's neck. "I'm not! I'm from the Bassa tribe!"

But the commando only shouted louder. "Yes, you are! I can tell by the look on your face! Look at you! You're so scared your eyes are popping from your skull!" He pointed a stabbing finger at Marbu and began to laugh wickedly as he shoved Marbu into the tall grass at the side of the road. "Eat grass!" he shouted like a maniac. "Eat grass, you beast!" and he put his foot on Marbu's head to push his face to the ground.

Marbu didn't try to argue with the man. It was horribly humiliating, but he grabbed mouthfuls of the grass in his mouth and began to chew on it.

"Eat more, I tell you!" The commando ground the heel of his army boot into the back of Marbu's neck.

Marbu shivered in horror to the depths of his soul. The commando sounded so evil, so satanic with fiendish delight at having Marbu in his power. How many victims like Marbu had he abused! How many innocent people had he already tortured and killed! It was almost incomprehensible that a human being could be so cruel, and yet Marbu knew it wasn't the soldier who was talking. It was a demonic force within him that was pushing him to harm those under his control. But there was nothing Marbu could do! He was totally helpless!

"Come with me!" The soldier suddenly dragged Marbu to his feet and pushed him toward a large tree. Marbu felt his knees grow weak. He wanted to run away in terror, but his legs would not cooperate! He was a lamb being led to the slaughter, and now he would die. After all the wearisome days on the road and all the painful hardships and prayers for deliverance, Marbu was going to be killed.

He had often imagined this moment of death. He had always thought of it as sometime, someplace far away from the real world in which he lived! He had always thought that when that day came, he would bow his head in humble acceptance of the hour of death that must come to every person born on this planet! He had thought he would face the ordeal like a man, ready to meet his Maker!

But nothing in his quiet contemplation of death had prepared him for the real thing! The real thing was now, and it was the most terrifying experience he had ever had!

Marbu stumbled, and the guard pushed him to his knees at the base of the tree. There around him were the bodies of others who had already been executed. He felt woozy, and his world began to spin around him at this ghastly atrocity! It was all so horrible and awful and wickedly appalling! For one bizarre moment Marbu's mind lifted him above the carnage of death surrounding him. For an instant he was able to step outside himself and contemplate the surrealness of what was happening to him. This mindless slaughter was all so wrong before God and humanity. Marbu was amazed that Charles Taylor and his soldiers couldn't see this senseless genocide for what it had become.

But there wasn't time to think on such things now; the commando had Marbu by the hair and was dragging him to the edge of a stream.

"You're one of Prince Johnson's men, aren't you!" he shouted.

"No, I'm not, I tell you! Please!" Marbu struggled to keep his footing. "I'm just a college student studying business classes!"

"Which town did you come from before you got here?" the commando grilled him.

Marbu was shaking so badly he could hardly think. "I-I-I-I don't know!" he stammered. "Waka, I think!"

"There! You see, I make my point!" The commando struck Marbu on the side of the head. "I hear that town is now under the control of Prince Johnson!"

"Yes, and that's why we left!" Marbu staggered and put his hands to his head to protect himself from a second blow. "We heard he was coming, and we wanted nothing to do with the man!"

"You lie, and I'm going to kill you for it!" The commando lifted the barrel of his machine gun and pointed it at Marbu.

"I am not the enemy! You're making a mistake!" Marbu screamed at the soldier in desperation. "If you kill me, it will be for nothing!" He was beside himself in anger and anguish, but he was worn out from trying to reason with this man.

Unfortunately, evil men sometimes cannot be reasoned with or bargained with for mercy. They are driven by the spirits of demons in the high places of wickedness. Marbu sensed this and finally gave up in despair. There was no longer any use in hoping for mercy! The commando was determined to kill Marbu, and that would be the end of it.

Marbu squeezed his eyes shut and waited for several torturous seconds. Then, unexpectedly, a famous passage of Scripture he had read a thousand times came to mind. Was there a Christian anywhere that didn't know the familiar lines?

"The Lord is my shepherd; I shall not want." The very thought of those

words had a calming effect on Marbu's mind and soul. He had not had the presence of mind to bring them up, so frightened was he. But somehow, unexplainably, they had come to him like the cool water of a rain shower on a hot summer's day.

"He makes me to lie down in green pastures; He leads me beside the still waters. He restores my soul; He leads me in the paths of righteousness for His name's sake." Marbu was in another world now, separated from the terror that had petrified him only seconds before. The panic that had frozen every muscle in his frightened body was now slowly ebbing away.

"Yea, though I walk through the valley of the shadow of death, I will fear no evil; for You are with me" (Ps. 23:1-4). The gun barrel was against his head, but Marbu knew he was not alone. God was with him here in the jungles of Liberia as he faced death at the hand of a cruel mercenary. In a moment it would all be over, and that was all right, Marbu reasoned. The next thing he would see would be Jesus coming in the clouds of heaven to take him home.

Marbu waited for several moments, and then heard the click of a firing pin in the AK-47, but there was no exploding pop of gunfire. No instant blackness of death he had expected would come. He knew something bizarre had happened, but he couldn't fully grasp what it was. And then it suddenly dawned on him that the gun hadn't gone off.

Click! Click! The commando pulled the trigger again. *Click, click, click,* but the rifle refused to fire, and the bullets would not come. Marbu stopped shaking.

Chapter 13

What is wrong with this stupid gun!" roared the commando, and a stream of cursing followed. He put the gun on safety and took it off again. He pulled the clip of shells from the gun and tried firing it again into the air, but the rifle seemed to be useless. Dropping the rifle, the commando ran down the bank of the stream and snatched a revolver from the holster of another soldier. Turning the revolver on Marbu, he pulled the trigger, but nothing happened. All he heard was the familiar *click, click*! The soldier opened the chamber to check if the bullet was in the gun, and then closed it again, aiming it at Marbu. Marbu closed his eyes again. Again he waited, and again the gun failed to fire.

Like a glimmer from a faint candle lighting a room, the assurance of God's presence began to creep over Marbu. Each momentary click of the gun Marbu thought would be his last, and yet a strange sense of calm was settling upon him. With every passing second he expected the path of a speeding bullet to hit him and end his life. But that moment did not come, and in its place was only peace. It was clear now to Marbu that guardian angels had been sent to protect him so that these commandos might not hurt him.

Marbu got up from the ground, convinced that God was preserving him. The whole ordeal should have been torturous for him, but it wasn't anymore. As the commando tried one gun and then another without success, a sudden realization struck Marbu's soul. This was exactly what the verse in Psalms was talking about—the shadow of death, and the fear of evil. Death might come, but it need not be feared, for God was with him.

By now the commando was crazy with demonic rage against this man who was defying death with such luck. Or so it seemed. Grabbing his machete, he charged up the streambed toward Marbu, swinging the machete around in the air. "Your voodoo powers may control my gun," he screamed, "but they're no match for my cutlass!"

For a moment Marbu panicked again, and then a strange thing happened. The commando swung the gleaming machete at Marbu's neck, but Marbu reached out and grabbed the man's arm with a viselike grip. Marbu was in control again with a strength he didn't know he had. The two of them struggled for several long moments, and then the commando finally dropped the machete to the ground. He stood there panting, glassy-eyed, his face a picture of surprise and confusion.

"What kind of black magic is it you have!" he demanded in angry fear. "You've got voodoo in you! I can feel the power surging through you! It's why my gun wouldn't fire!"

"I have no voodoo," Marbu said, breathing hard. "I'm a Christian! God is my power!"

"You're lying, and I can prove it!" the commando growled, and he grabbed at Marbu's shirt. "You've got the marks of voodoo on your chest or back!" He yanked at Marbu's shirt, ripping it from his shoulders. But of course there were no ritual marks of voodoo on Marbu's body.

Snatching up the machete again, the commando took another swing at Marbu, and this time Marbu had to duck. But he grabbed the back of the soldier's wrist before he could swing the machete again, and once again the struggle was on.

"I'm going to kill you if it's the last thing I do!" screamed the commando. "Your powers can't last forever!"

Marbu knew he was struggling with more than just a man. There was a demon in this commando, and it had taken hold of his soul. He was more physically fit than Marbu and far stronger, so he should have easily been able to overwhelm Marbu, and yet he couldn't. God was keeping Marbu, protecting him from the evil powers of the supernatural world. *Help me, Lord!* Marbu found himself praying. The answer came once again in quite an unexpected form.

At that moment a big black car drove up to the checkpoint, and a rather distinguished military man got out. "Soldier!" he shouted as he spotted Marbu and the commando struggling. "Bring that man over to the checkpoint!"

Marbu grabbed the machete out of the commando's hand and threw it into the jungle. The commando shrugged at the officer's order, but of course he had no choice. He had to obey. Marbu tried to catch his breath as he stared at the officer standing near the car. The man had to be one of Charles Taylor's senior military men, wearing that uniform and riding in that type of car. Another colonel? A general, maybe?

The commando gestured toward the checkpoint. "Let's go!" he barked, but Marbu refused to lead the way, fearing the man might try to stab him in the back with another weapon.

The commando shrugged and finally led the way, leaving his machine gun and machete behind. When they reached the checkpoint, the commando began shouting at Marbu again, accusing him of being a spy for Prince Johnson, that he was a tribal Krahn, and that he had family members working for Samuel Doe in the government.

Marbu listened to the charges with mounting fear. He was grateful for a few more moments of life, but he had to wonder what would come next. He had no idea really who this high-ranking military man was, but his fate certainly rested in the officer's hands. That the officer had come just when Marbu needed him was no secret. But what would the officer do now that he had heard the accusations? Would he agree with the commando's trumped-up charges? Would he order Marbu to be executed on the spot?

It was a moment of tense waiting, and Marbu felt himself beginning to panic once again. How many more ways could a man suffer and die? he wondered. He had been shot at in his own house back in Paynesville, had suffered from heat exhaustion in the sun while waiting to be interrogated, and then bitten by malaria-infested mosquitoes each night. He had avoided enemy patrols, rockets, and ambush. He had escaped certain death by guns and a machete at the hands of a demon-possessed commando! What more could the devil throw at him?

The high-ranking officer looked to be a busy man, but he finally turned to Marbu at the commando's insistence. "Who are you, son? What are you doing here?"

Marbu tried to look as sincere as he knew how. "My name is Marbu Watkins, and I'm a student," he said slowly. "I'm not a Krahn, and I don't have any relatives who work for Doe in his government."

The officer listened to Marbu for a few more minutes, and then gave his verdict. "This man is not our enemy. You may go," he said to Marbu as he sent him on his way with a wave of his hand.

Marbu stood staring at the officer for a moment longer, but only a moment. He didn't want to give the man a chance to change his mind. Otis and James joined him as they all passed the checkpoint gate, and then they quickly headed off down the road. Where they were going, they didn't know, but they didn't care. Marbu was still alive, and so were Otis and James. One thing was for sure. With God along to protect them, they didn't really need to worry anymore.

As Marbu and his friends put distance between themselves and Todee Junction, they began to breathe more easily. The sun was still hot, and the open road offered no shelter from approaching night, but Marbu felt free as a bird. He had stared death in the face once again and lived to tell about it. The odds of life and death had been against him, but by God's miraculous grace he had won. Then again, should he have been surprised? God had walked with Marbu through the shadows of death. He had been Marbu's refuge and strength, a help in times of trouble.

Marbu stared up at the bright afternoon sky as if he somehow expected to see the face of God among the clouds. *Thank You, Lord,* he breathed in gratefulness. *Your goodness and mercy have followed me every step of this journey, Lord, and I have no doubt You will follow me all the days of my life. What a grand story the angels will tell when I finally see You face to face.*

Epilogue

During the remainder of their trip, Marbu, Otis, and James became very close. Otis admired Marbu for his faith in God and seemed eager to learn more from the Bible. Marbu's brother James had never been much of a believer either, but with all their near-death experiences, he found enough reasons to seek God with all his heart.

The next morning the high-ranking officer happened to drive by the three boys on the road and stopped to talk with them. Surprisingly, he offered them transport in the back of a dump truck on its way to the coastal city of Buchanan, a neutral city thought to be safer for refugees. Marbu and his traveling buddies gratefully accepted the invitation. Until now all their traveling had been on foot. The ride in the truck was the first of its kind since they left Paynesville more than three weeks before.

When they arrived in Buchanan, Otis took Marbu and James to the home of his aunt and uncle. The elderly couple opened their hearts to the boys, but they became especially fond of Marbu. Like Otis, they were attracted to Marbu's dynamic testimony, and his faith experience with God, and soon he was part of their family. Every morning and evening it became Marbu's habit to read the Bible with them and pray. They loved these quiet times with God's Word and the verses of Scripture Marbu recited so enthusiastically.

Before the war in Liberia had thrown Marbu's life into chaos, he had been studying business and accounting so he could go into business for himself. Now he realized he had a much bigger work to do. He needed to share his story of faith and deliverance. He needed to go to school to become a minister. The Adventist Seminary of West Africa* in Nigeria seemed like the answer to his dreams, but getting there would be a problem. He had very little in worldly possesions, and money was not high on the list.

Through a series of God-given opportunities and miraculous faith experiences, Marbu and a friend arrived in a refugee camp just across the border in Côte d'Ivoire. Unfortunately, Marbu didn't have the proper papers to travel, or to qualify him for a scholarship. And then to top it all off, the little bit of money he did have was stolen by a man who took advantage of him when he helped him get medical treatment in the refugee camp. Marbu was in a strange country with no money. He was clearly near the end of his proverbial rope. However, he steadfastly held to his faith in God and the memory of his miraculous deliverance in Liberia. He prayed fervently that God would once again intervene and show him the way, but he had no idea how this might happen.

And then God's providence smiled on him once more. A missionary family in Abidjan, Côte d'Ivoire, offered to sponsor Marbu's traveling expenses and one year's tuition at the Adventist Seminary in Nigeria. Marbu was ecstatic as he realized that God had again delivered him out of his distress.

He had suffered incredible hardship at the hands of Satan and the ruthless Liberian revolutionaries, but he had escaped from behind enemy lines. Now he was on his way to be trained as a minister of the gospel. No longer would he study accounting and business. From this day forward his only business would be to prepare others for the kingdom of God.

---

* The Adventist Seminary of West Africa in Nigeria (ASWA) has since been renamed Babcock University after an American missionary named David Babcock, who pioneered the work of Seventh-day Adventists in Nigeria in 1914.

More Exciting Miracle Stories

The Seventh-day Ox and Other Miracle Stories From Russia
Bradley Booth

The Seventh-day Ox and Other Miracle Stories From Russia describes the faithfulness of Christians during times of persecution and the animals who were used by God to help them. Against all odds, each of these witnesses placed their trust in God and demonstrated unbroken commitment to their faith—no matter what the cost. 978-0-8280-2517-1

Availability subject to change.

An Amazing Story of Faith

Like Daniel of old, when the regulations of his country clashed with the laws of God, Ivan Gumenyuk chose to stand alone.

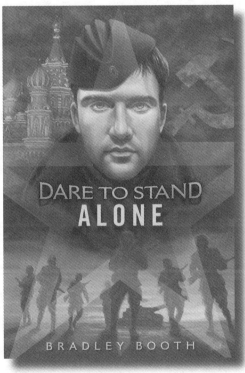

Dare to Stand Alone
Bradley Booth

This is the riveting true story of a teenage boy who found the courage to stand up and speak boldly about his God—in the Soviet Army. Foolish? Maybe. Risky? Definitely. 978-0-8127-0457-0. Paperback, 128 pages.